Ambient Findability

Other resources from O'Reilly

Related titles
Practical RDF   Google Maps Hacks
Mapping Hacks   Designing Interfaces
Google Hacks   Web Design in a Nutshell

oreilly.com
oreilly.com is more than a complete catalog of O'Reilly books. You'll also find links to news, events, articles, weblogs, sample chapters, and code examples.

oreillynet.com is the essential portal for developers interested in open and emerging technologies, including new platforms, programming languages, and operating systems.

Conferences
O'Reilly brings diverse innovators together to nurture the ideas that spark revolutionary industries. We specialize in documenting the latest tools and systems, translating the innovator's knowledge into useful skills for those in the trenches. Visit *conferences.oreilly.com* for our upcoming events.

Safari Bookshelf (*safari.oreilly.com*) is the premier online reference library for programmers and IT professionals. Conduct searches across more than 1,000 books. Subscribers can zero in on answers to time-critical questions in a matter of seconds. Read the books on your Bookshelf from cover to cover or simply flip to the page you need. Try it today for free.

Ambient Findability

Peter Morville

O'REILLY®

Beijing · Cambridge · Farnham · Köln · Paris · Sebastopol · Taipei · Tokyo

005.72
MORVILLE, P

Ambient Findability

by Peter Morville

3 1257 01615 2240

Published by O'Reilly Media, Inc., 1005 Gravenstein Highway North, Sebastopol, CA 95472.

O'Reilly books may be purchased for educational, business, or sales promotional use. Online editions are also available for most titles (*safari.oreilly.com*). For more information, contact our corporate/institutional sales department: (800) 998-9938 or *corporate@oreilly.com*.

Editor:	Simon St.Laurent
Production Editor:	Adam Witwer
Cover Designer:	Karen Montgomery
Interior Designer:	David Futato

Printing History:

September 2005: First Edition.

 This book uses RepKover,™ a durable and flexible lay-flat binding.

ISBN: 0-596-00765-5
[C]

[11/05*]

For Claire and Claudia

Table of Contents

About the Author

Peter Morville is president of Semantic Studios, an information architecture and findability consultancy. For over a decade, he has advised such clients as AT&T, IBM, Microsoft, Harvard Business School, Internet2, Procter & Gamble, Vanguard, and Yahoo!. Peter is best known as a founding father of information architecture, having coauthored the field's best-selling book, *Information Architecture for the World Wide Web*.

Figure P-1. Peter Morville

Peter serves on the faculty at the University of Michigan's School of Information and on the advisory board of the Information Architecture Institute. He delivers keynotes and seminars at international events, and his work has been featured in major publications, including *Business Week*, *The Economist*, *Fortune*, and *The Wall Street Journal*.

You can contact Peter Morville by email (*morville@semanticstudios.com*). You can also find him offline at 42.2° N 83.4° W or online at *semanticstudios.com* and *findability.org*.

Preface

How did you get here? This is not a metaphysical or genealogical inquiry. I'm not interested in your spiritual beliefs, and I'm certainly not barking up your family tree. My question is both practical and relevant. How did you find this book? Perhaps you stumbled across it in a library or bookstore or at the end of a keyword search on ubiquitous computing or wayfinding or experience design or decision making.

What were you looking for? What words did you use? That's what I want to know. Or did this book find you? Is it a gift from a friend or a required textbook in your marketing management class? Is someone making you read it? Perhaps they want you to learn about web design or social software or artificial intelligence or evolutionary psychology.

I ask because the odds of finding this book are vanishingly small. Estimates place the worldwide stock of books between 75 and 175 million titles; plus there are millions of blogs, billions of web pages, countless radio and TV shows, RSS feeds, podcasts, and the beat goes on. Most folks are more likely to win the lottery than find this book.

So, what's this book about? That's a tough one. I could tell you it's about information interaction at the crossroads of mobile computing and the Internet, or claim it opens a window onto the singular cultural revolution of our time. I could invite you to look up its Library of Congress subject headings or its Statistically Improbable Phrases in Amazon. But I won't. Instead, I'll ask you to read it, for *aboutness* lies in the eye of the beholder.

Who's this book for? Another stumper. I might classify the target audiences as designers, engineers, teachers, anthropologists, and librarians, but that leaves out students, artists, comedians, and business executives. I could declare it's for anyone who's ever been lost or wanted to be found, but that sounds corny. I might say it's for everyone. But I won't. Instead, I'll ask you to read this book, figure out who it's for, and send them a copy.

Organization of This Book

This book should be read in linear style from start to end. You should not need a map. But just in case you wander off the path, we've embedded some wayfinding devices. Each page has a number. Each chapter has a name. There's an alphabetical index and a hierarchical table of contents. And, if that's not enough, here's a brief topical guide:

Preface (You Are Here!)
Identifies the scope, purpose, organization, conventions, and target audiences. Tells you how to contact the author and publisher. Includes an introduction and acknowledgments.

Chapter 1, *Lost and Found*
Explains findability and findable objects with definitions, examples, and stories. Explores the value and values of ambient findability. Keywords: Treo, GPS, RFID, Long Tail.

Chapter 2, *A Brief History of Wayfinding*
Connects animal and human navigation in natural and built environments to transmedia wayfinding in the 21st century. Keywords: Turtles, Labyrinths, Maps, Myst, Metaphor.

Chapter 3, *Information Interaction*
Exposes the long now of information-seeking behavior through the hard lens of evolutionary psychology. Keywords: Power Laws, Relevance, False Drops, Gossip.

Chapter 4, *Intertwingled*
Explores findability, findable objects, and wayfinding at the wavefront of ubiquitous computing and corporal convergence. Keywords: Ingestibles, Everyware, Privacy.

Chapter 5, *Push and Pull*
Describes how findability and the Web are transforming the marketplace and reshaping the rules of marketing. Keywords: Bananas, Spam, Search Costs, Personalization.

Chapter 6, *The Sociosemantic Web*
Bridges the gap between social software and the Semantic Web by placing ontologies, taxonomies, and folksonomies into context. Keywords: Tags, Popularity, Authority.

Chapter 7, *Inspired Decisions*
Concludes with a safari through the tangled hierarchies of artificial intelligence, irrational decision making, and human behavior. Keywords: Mazes, Memory, Neocortex, Colour.

Safari Enabled

 When you see a Safari® Enabled icon on the cover of your favorite technology book, it means the book is available online through the O'Reilly Network Safari Bookshelf.

Safari offers a solution that's better than e-books. It's a virtual library that lets you easily search thousands of top technology books, cut and paste code samples, download chapters, and find quick answers when you need the most accurate, current information. Try it for free at *http://safari.oreilly.com*.

Contacting the Author

Please send questions and comments (and compliments) to Peter Morville:

> Email: *morville@semanticstudios.com*
> Web: *http://semanticstudios.com*
> Blog: *http://findability.org*

Contacting O'Reilly

Comments and questions can also be addressed to the publisher:

> O'Reilly Media, Inc.
> 1005 Gravenstein Highway North
> Sebastopol, CA 95472
> (800) 998-9938 (in the United States or Canada)
> (707) 829-0515 (international or local)
> (707) 829-0104 (fax)

We have a web page for this book, where we list errata, examples, and any additional information. You can access this page at:

> *http://www.oreilly.com/catalog/ambient*

To comment or ask technical questions about this book, send email to:

> *bookquestions@oreilly.com*

For more information about our books, conferences, Resource Centers, and the O'Reilly Network, see our web site: *http://www.oreilly.com*.

Acknowledgments

First, I wish to thank Susan. You are a wonderful wife, a great librarian, a fabulous cook, and a truly amazing mom. Thanks for your support and patience. I will always love you.

I'd also like to recognize Louis Rosenfeld and Joseph Janes for introducing me to the Internet, and for launching the vessel we called Argus. And thanks to all the Argonauts who made the journey fun. You're right, Dennis. The ship was lost, but not the people.

I'm indebted to my technical reviewers: Adam Greenfield, Chris Farnum, Christina Wodtke, Dan Klyn, Gene Smith, Paul Morville, Peter Bogaards, Peter Merholz, Samantha Bailey, Scott Hauman, Tom Rieke, Shelley Powers, and Victor Lombardi. Thanks!

I thank my clients at the National Cancer Institute, my colleagues at Q LTD, and my friends in the field who bring the communities of ASIST and IAI to life. I thank my sister, Rosalind Morville, for her sage PR advice, and my parents, Malcolm and Judith.

Finally, I thank the Web, which connects me to countless sources of inspiration, and perpetually changes both my journey and my destination.

CHAPTER 1

Lost and Found

At the seashore, between the land of atoms
and the sea of bits, we are now facing the
challenge of reconciling our dual citizenship
in the physical and digital worlds.
—Hiroshi Ishii
MIT Media Lab

I'm sitting on a beach in Newport, Rhode Island. Seagulls and sandpipers hunt near the water's edge. The Atlantic ocean sparkles in the early morning sun. To my right, the Cliff Walk winds its way between the rugged New England shoreline and the manicured gardens of the Newport mansions, opulent "summer cottages" built with industrial age fortunes made in steamships, railroads, and foreign trade.

I'm sitting on a beach in Newport, but I'm not entirely there. My attention is focused on a device that rests in the palm of my hand. It's a Treo 600 smartphone. I'm using it to write this sentence, right here, right now. As a 6.2 ounce computer sporting a 144 megahertz RISC processor, 32 megabytes of RAM, a color display, and a full QWERTY keyboard, this is one impressive micro-machine. But that's not what floats my boat. What I love about this device is its ability to reach out *beyond* the here and now.

By integrating a mobile phone and Palm Powered organizer with wireless email, text messaging, and web browsing, the Treo connects me with global communication and information networks. I can make a phone call, send email, check the weather, buy a book, learn about Newport, and find a restaurant for lunch. The whole world is accessible and addressable through this 21st Century looking glass in the palm of my hands.

But make no mistake, this device is a two-way mirror. Not only can people reach out and touch me with a phone call, an email, or a text message.

Equipped with the right technology, someone could pinpoint my location within a few hundred feet. Like most new smartphones, my Treo includes an embedded Global Positioning System chip designed to support E911 emergency location services. In other words, I'm findable.

Here's where things get interesting. We're at an inflection point in the evolution of findability. We're creating all sorts of new interfaces and devices to access information, and we're simultaneously importing tremendous volumes of information about people, places, products, and possessions into our ubiquitous digital networks.

Consider the following examples:

- There's a company called Ambient Devices that embeds information representation into everyday objects: lights, pens, watches, walls, and wearables. You can buy a wireless Ambient Orb that shifts colors to show changes in the weather, stock market, and traffic patterns based on user preferences you set on a web site.

- From the highways of Seattle and Los Angeles to the city streets of Tokyo and Berlin, embedded wireless sensors and real-time data services for mobile devices are enabling motorists to learn about and route around traffic jams and accidents.

- Pioneers in "convergent architecture" have built the Swisshouse, a new type of consulate in Cambridge, Massachussetts that connects a geographically dispersed scientific community. It may not be long before persistent audio-video linkages and "web on the wall" come to a building near you.

- Delicious Library's social software turns an iMac and FireWire digital video camera into a multimedia cataloging system. Simply scan the barcode on any book, movie, music, or video game, and the item's cover appears on your digital shelves along with tons of information from the Web. This sexy, location-aware, peer-to-peer, personal lending library lets you share your collection with friends and neighbors.

- You can buy a watch from Wherify Wireless with an integrated global positioning system (GPS) that locks onto your kid's wrist, so you can pinpoint his location at any time. A nifty "breadcrumb" feature shows where your child has wandered over the course of several hours. Similar devices are available in amusement parks such as Denmark's Legoland, so parents can quickly find their lost children.

- Manufacturers such as Procter & Gamble have already begun inserting radio-frequency identification tags (RFIDs) into products so they can reduce theft and restock shelves more efficiently. These tags continue to function long after products leave the store and enter the home or business.

- At the Baja Beach Club in Barcelona, patrons can buy drinks and open doors with a wave of their hand, compliments of a syringe-injected, RFID microchip implant. The system knows who you are, where you are, and your exact credit balance. Getting "chipped" is considered a luxury service, available for VIP members only.

The size and price of processors, sensors, radio frequency identification tags, and related technologies are approaching a tipping point. Today's expensive prototypes are tomorrow's dirt cheap products. Imagine the ability to track the location of anyone or anything from anywhere at anytime. Simply affix a tiny sticker to your TV's remote control or to the bottom of your spouse's shoe, and then fire up your Treo's web browser.

We're stepping through the looking glass into an information-rich world with new possibilities and problems. We will find delight in groovy gadgets and location-based services. Individuals and institutions will achieve greater flexibility and productivity. And yet, we will struggle to balance privacy, freedom, convenience, and safety.

And amidst all this novelty, our vaunted ability to "learn how to learn" will be put to the test. How will we make informed decisions? How will we know enough to ask the right questions? Nine billion web pages. Six billion people. Who do you ask? Who do you trust? How do you find the best product, the right person, the data that makes a difference?

The answers are hidden in the strange connections between wayfinding, social software, information retrieval, decision trees, self-organization, evolutionary psychology, librarianship, and authority. As William Gibson, the science-fiction author who coined the term *cyberspace*, once noted, "The future exists today. It's just unevenly distributed."

Where the Internet meets ubiquitous computing, the histories of navigation, communication, commerce, and information seeking converge. We increasingly use mobile devices to find our way, to find products, to find answers, and to find ourselves. As we map the emerging shoreline that connects the land of atoms and the sea of bits, *findability* serves as a useful lens for seeing where we've been and what lies ahead.

Definition

At this point, you may be wondering: what exactly is findability? This section is for you.

find·a·bil·i·ty *n*

    a. The quality of being locatable or navigable.

    b. The degree to which a particular object is easy to discover or locate.

    c. The degree to which a system or environment supports navigation and retrieval.

Findability is a quality that can be measured at both the object and system levels. We can study the attributes of an individual object that make it more or less findable. The title of a document. The color of a life jacket. The presence of an embedded RFID tag. And we can evaluate how well an overall system supports people's ability to find their way and find what they need. Can patients navigate a hospital? Can users navigate a web site?

Of course, the successes of findable objects and their systems are often closely linked. An orange life jacket fails to grab attention in an orange ocean, but a statistically improbable phrase jumps right out in a sea of books. Findability requires definition, distinction, difference. In physical environments, size, shape, color, and location set objects apart. In the digital realm, we rely heavily on words. Words as labels. Words as links. Keywords.

The humble keyword has become surprisingly important in recent years. As a vital ingredient in the online search process, keywords have become part of our everyday experience. We feed keywords into Google, Yahoo!, MSN, eBay, and Amazon. We search for news, products, people, used furniture, and music. And words are the key to our success.

The power of the keyword search has combined with the richness of the World Wide Web to foment a revolution in the way we do business. This revolution is not simply about moving the shopping experience online. It's about empowering individuals with information and choice. Never before has the consumer had so much access to product information *before* the point of purchase. Never before have we had so many products to choose from. Power has shifted and continues to shift toward the consumer.

As the pendulum swings from push to pull, the effectiveness of advertising diminishes relative to the importance of product design and quality and price. No longer forced to trust the promotional spin of television advertisements and predatory salespeople, we now have the ability to find the best products and the best deals. We can make informed decisions, thanks to the simple keyword and our sophisticated engines of findability.

For when you examine the tools and systems available for finding and evaluating products, keyword search is only the beginning. Consider the richness of Amazon, where we can compare and contrast myriad products in amazing detail. The hunt starts with a keyword search or perhaps the choice of category and subcategory.

Let's say we're looking for a digital camera. We choose *Electronics*, then *Camera and Photo*, then *Digital Cameras*. Now the selection really begins. We can browse by brand or filter by megapixel range. We can focus on the bestsellers or the lowest prices. For any given camera, we can view descriptions and specifications from the manufacturer, and weigh their claims against the color commentary of customer reviews.

> This camera is awesome! That camera sucks! There's no tripod mount. You can't recharge the battery overseas. This one's too small for people with big hands. Try this one instead. I dropped mine in a pond but it still works perfectly fine.

These customer reviews are funny, insightful, and valuable, yet they also force us to play a more active role in evaluating our sources of information. Who do we trust? Amazon? The manufacturer? Some random customer? We need to validate claims by cross-reference, so we check out Epinions, CNET, and Consumer Reports. And if possible, we ask a friend. All of these sources and our own judgments about their trustworthiness and credibility inform the process of finding the right product.

The credibility and authority of sources become even more important when we step into the arena of health information. In an age of skyrocketing health care costs and doctors with little time to spare, we are taking our questions online. In the United States, 80% of adult Internet users, or almost half of Americans over the age of 18 (about 95 million individuals) have researched health and medical topics on the Internet. We learn about specific diseases. We educate ourselves about medical procedures. We search for nutritional supplements. And we seek alternative treatments and medicines for ourselves and for our loved ones. In the process, our literacy is put to the test. Can we find what we seek? Can we evaluate what we do find? Are our decisions getting better or worse?

I can tell you from personal experience that Google does not perform well when it comes to health. Recently, our youngest daughter, Claudia, was diagnosed with a severe peanut allergy. Suddenly interested in a topic I had never cared about before, I turned to the Web for answers. Google sent me to specialized sites such as *peanutallergy.com*, a shallow and grossly commercial web site pushing favored brands of nut free chocolate and soy-nut butter. Yahoo! and MSN didn't perform any better. I did eventually find what I needed, but only by drawing on my advanced searching skills and familiarity with authoritative sources like the National Institutes of Health and the Centers for Disease Control. If I weren't a librarian who lives on the Web, I would have failed to find the right answers.

Sometimes the health information we find online validates our doctor's diagnosis or advice. Sometimes it sends us for a second opinion. And sometimes it simply makes us feel better informed and more confident. Consider the following excerpt from an email message sent to the National Cancer Institute:

> Last evening I learned my 72 yr. old mother has lung cancer. Still in a state of shock she was not able to provide me with much information. She lives four hours from me and I am unable to be with her at this moment due to work obligations. So until I can be with her I am taking the time to learn as much as possible on the subject of lung cancer. So I would like to thank the person or persons for this very informative web site. This web site has given me the information on how I as a daughter can help my mother and also teach my family what to expect in the next coming months. Thank you!

In this message of grief and gratitude, we can find hope and inspiration. Hope in the reality of progress. The sender couldn't have found what she needed only a few years ago. Though we already take it for granted, the Internet is still the fastest growing new medium of all time. And inspiration in understanding that the work we do to connect people with content and services and one another truly makes a difference. Designers, developers, writers, and others who labor behind the screens to shape the user experience rarely get to see the personal impact of their work. We maintain *empathy for the user* as a matter of faith. Messages from and contact with our users help us to renew that faith.

Of course, the user experience is increasingly *out of control*, as wireless devices inject new interfaces and affordances into an already complex network ecology. How do we design for mobility? How do we create good experiences when we can't predict context of use? Will our users be in the office or in the bathtub? What's their bandwidth and screen size? The variables will only multiply as ubicomp transforms the Web into both interface and infrastructure for an ambient Internet of objects we can barely imagine.

> **am·bi·ent** *adj*
>
> a. Surrounding; encircling: *e.g., ambient sound.*
>
> b. Completely enveloping.

Ambient findability describes a fast emerging world where we can find anyone or anything from anywhere at anytime. We're not there yet, but we're headed in the right direction. Information is in the air, literally. And it changes our minds, physically. Most importantly, findability invests freedom in the individual. As the Web challenges mass media with a media of the masses, we will enjoy an unprecented ability to select our sources and choose our news. In my opinion, findability is going ambient, just in time.

Information Literacy

The average child in the United States watches four hours of television every day. These kids are exposed to 20,000 commercials annually. They see 8,000 onscreen murders by the time they finish grade school. Is this a good thing? As a society, we send mixed signals. On the one hand, we condemn the evils of television. Authorities such as the American Academy of Pediatrics warn that TV viewing may lead to more aggressive behavior, less physical activity, and risky sexual behavior. Newspaper headlines blame television for our epidemics of violence, obesity, and illiteracy. And yet, we let our children watch it. Perhaps we question the authorities and doubt the headlines. Perhaps we lack the time or energy to intervene. Or perhaps we trust that things will be okay because all the other kids are watching too. Perhaps.

Whenever I hear about the dominance of television and the decline of literacy, I experience a disconnect. While I do fear for the health of this media-saturated generation, I don't worry about their ability to read and write. Our culture does not reward illiteracy. On the contrary, it's almost impossible to function in modern society without mastering the skills of written communication. If you can't fill out a form, you're in trouble. The literacy rate in the United States is 97%. It's 99% throughout most of Europe. Basic literacy is not in danger. However, it's also not enough.

Our children are inheriting a media landscape that's breathtaking and bewildering. Books, magazines, newspapers, billboards, telephones, televisions, videotapes, video games, email messages, text messages, instant messages, web sites, weblogs, wikis, and the list goes on. It's exciting to have all these communication tools and information sources at our disposal, but the complexity of the environment demands new kinds of literacy. Gone are the days when we can look up the "right answer" in the family encyclopedia. Nowadays there are many answers in many places. We can find them in Microsoft Encarta or in the Wikipedia. We can find them via Google. There is so much to find, but we must first know how to search and who to trust. In the information age, transmedia information literacy is a core life skill.

The American Library Association defines information literacy as "a set of abilities requiring individuals to recognize when information is needed and have the ability to locate, evaluate, and use effectively the needed information."

> Information literacy also is increasingly important in the contemporary environment of rapid technological change and proliferating information resources. Because of the escalating complexity of this environment, individuals are faced with diverse, abundant information choices—in their academic studies, in the workplace, and in their personal lives. Information is available through libraries, community resources, special interest organizations, media, and the Internet—and increasingly, information comes to individuals in unfiltered formats, raising questions about its authenticity, validity, and reliability. In addition, information is available through multiple media, including graphical, aural, and textual, and these pose new challenges for individuals in evaluating and understanding it. The uncertain quality and expanding quantity of information pose large challenges for society. The sheer abundance of information will not in itself create a more informed citizenry without a complementary cluster of abilities necessary to use information effectively.[*]

Information literacy helps individuals succeed. As consumers, fluency with the use of multiple media enables us to find the best products at the best prices more efficiently. Whether you're buying a book or a car or a house, the Internet can often save you significant time and money. As producers, information literacy helps us find and keep the best jobs. Knowledge workers are paid for their ability to find, filter, analyze, create, and otherwise manage information. Those who lack these skills become lost on the wrong side of the digital divide. As a society, we must continue to invest in the education of our children, and we must work harder to develop information literacy among our citizens.

Business Value

Let's say you're unmoved by the idealistic call for greater literacy. Our children may be our future, but you've got budget problems and business challenges today. Why should you care about findability? Why should you learn more about social software, semantic webs, and search engine optimization? What can findability do for you?

We begin our quest for business value in the unlikely domain of a federal government agency. Yes, we're back at the National Cancer Institute where I recently had the good fortune to collaborate with a great team of people on redesigning the *cancer.gov* web site. I was brought in to lead the informa-

---

[*] Information Literacy Competency Standards. American Library Association: *http://www.ala.org/ala/acrl/acrlstandards/informationliteracycompetency.htm*.

tion architecture strategy. My goals were to improve navigation and usability, and reduce the number of clicks required to access key content.

The in-house team at NCI had done a great job analyzing patterns of use. They understood who visits, why they visit, and where they spend their time. They knew the majority of site visitors are people recently diagnosed with cancer (and their friends and family members). And their data showed the home pages for specific types of cancer were among the most visited. So, among other goals, they wanted to reduce the time and number of clicks it took to navigate from the NCI home page to cancer type home pages.

Now, being a findability fanatic, I couldn't help inquiring about how people find the web site in the first place. My clients didn't have much data on this topic, but they told me not to worry about this type of findability. Our site comes up as the first or second hit for searches on "cancer" on Google and Yahoo! they told me, so we're all set.

But I did worry, and I did a bit of digging. I used Overture's Search Term Suggestion Tool to get a sense of the types of cancer-related searches being performed on public search engines. Sure enough, the generic query on "cancer" was the single most popular search (i.e., 180,000 queries per month). But queries on specific types of cancer were also very common (e.g., 132,000 on "breast cancer" per month). In fact, when you totaled the searches on specific types of cancer, they outnumbered the generic searches by a 5:1 ratio, as Figure 1-1 shows. This makes sense. If you're diagnosed with breast cancer, you're very likely to search on "breast cancer" rather than explore the more general category of cancer.

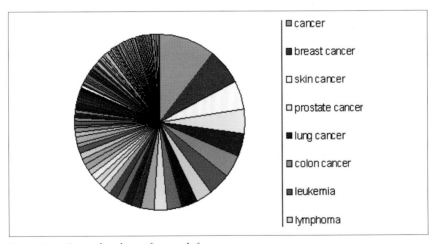

Figure 1-1. General and specific search frequency

Yet when I tried Google and Yahoo! searches on "breast cancer" and "prostate cancer" and "mesothelioma," *cancer.gov* didn't come up in the first screen of results. It was drowned out by a multitude of more specialized, more commercial, less detailed, less trustworthy web sites. For users with these specific queries, the NCI site, shown in Figure 1-2, was essentially *unfindable*. In my opinion, this was a major problem. In fact, I told my clients that if they had to choose between having me redesign the information architecture and having a search engine optimization firm improve cancer type home page visibility for the most important and common cancer-related keyword searches, I'd recommend the latter.

Fortunately, my clients weren't forced to choose. In fact, we worked together on a holistic findability strategy to make it easier for users to find the site, to find the site's content, and to find their way around the site. And, in the year since this *cancer.gov* redesign, the National Cancer Institute has won a *Webby Award* and a *Freddie Award* and has climbed to the very top of the American Customer Satisfaction Index for E-Government. This goes to show that good things happen when you focus on findability.

But why hadn't my clients identified and solved their findability problems sooner? Because, like so many other design teams, they viewed their responsibility from a top-down perspective. Can users find what they need from the home page? It's an important question, but it ignores the fact that many users don't start from the home page. Powerful search tools, directories, blogs, social bookmarks, and syndication services are moving deep linking and content sampling from exception to rule. Many of your users will never visit your home page. And some may not even realize the answers they want are on the Web. People often assume they'll have to visit a library or ask a professional, and for lack of time or money, they get stuck. Can users find what they need from wherever they are? That's the multi-channel communication question we should be asking.

At NCI, the team had to look beyond the narrow goals of web site design, to see their role in advancing the broader mission of disseminating cancer information to people in need. They had a blind spot when it came to findability, and it's a weakness shared by many if not most organizations today. Executives want a web site that looks good. And thankfully, most now want a web site that's usable. But few executives understand the Web and how people use it well enough to recognize the vital importance of findability.

This is no small oversight. In a marketplace that's shifting from push to pull, findability is a big deal. As a pioneer of Internet search engine advertising, Overture recognized this opportunity early and capitalized on it to the tune of $1.6 billion (the value of their acquisition by Yahoo!). Paco Underhill, the

Figure 1-2. The National Cancer Institute's home page

guru of the science of shopping, acknowledges this transition in his best-selling book, *Why We Buy*:

> Generations ago, the commercial messages intended for consumers' ears came in highly concentrated, reliable form. There were three TV networks, AM radio only, a handful of big-circulation national magazines and each town's daily papers, which all adults read. Big brand-name goods were advertised in those media, and the message got through loud, clear and dependably. Today, we have remote controls and VCRs to allow us to skip all the ads if we choose to. There's FM radio now, a plethora of magazines catering to each little special interest, a World Wide Web of infinitely expanding sites we can visit for information and entertainment and a shrinking base of newspaper readers, all of which means it is harder to reach consumers and convince them to buy anything at all.[*]

---

[*] *Why We Buy* by Paco Underhill. Simon & Schuster (1999), p. 31–32.

In a world where it's getting harder to reach consumers, shouldn't businesses make it easier for consumers to reach them? Yet, when it comes to findability, most business web sites have major problems. Poor information architecture. Weak compliance with web standards. No metadata. Content buried in databases that are invisible to search engines. From sales to support, many firms could get a great return by investing in findability.

But the fault lines extend well beyond web design. Findability is transforming the marketplace. For those who pay attention, the signals of tectonic shift are self-evident in what Chris Anderson of *Wired* calls the Long Tail, shown in Figure 1-3. In his colorful analysis of the "millions of niche markets at the shallow end of the bitstream," Anderson explains how the virtually unlimited selection of online catalogs is shaking up our economy:

> What's really amazing about the Long Tail is the sheer size of it. Combine enough non-hits on the Long Tail and you've got a market bigger than hits. Take books: the average Barnes & Noble carries 130,000 titles. Yet more than half of Amazon's book sales come from outside its top 130,000 titles. Consider the implication...the market for books that are not even sold in the average bookstore is larger than the market for those that are.[*][†]

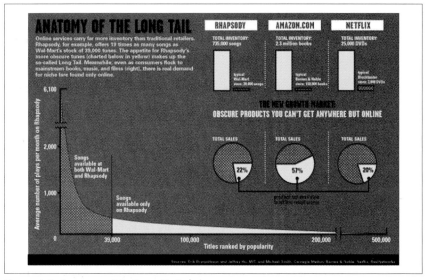

Figure 1-3. Anatomy of the Long Tail

---

[*] "The Long Tail" by Chris Anderson. Available at *http://www.wired.com/wired/archive/12.10/tail.html*.

[†] On August 3, 2005, Chris Anderson retracted his estimate that 57% of Amazon's book sales are in the Long Tail. Current estimates are in the less shocking but still impressive 25%–40% range. For the full story, see *http://longtail.typepad.com/the_long_tail/2005/08/a_methodology_f.html*.

As venture capitalist Kevin Laws puts it: "The biggest money is in the smallest sales." In an economy where it takes almost nothing to produce and stock one more item, the competitive challenges and big wins are in findability. How do we reduce search costs and time to find? How do we use social software to drive demand down the Long Tail?

Amazon, eBay, Google, iTunes, and Netflix are all Long Tail. Each of these early adopters uses search in support of mass customization. They know you can't buy what you can't find. And they understand this is a tail that will ultimately wag the dog. How will your business respond? The search space is huge. The potential for top line growth is big. But you better jump now while there's still plenty of room at the bottom.*

But wait. Don't move too fast. Or you just might wander off a cliff. In matters of findability, the siren song of technology has lured many to destruction. Though our attention is drawn to the fast layers of hi-tech, the map to this maze is buried in the slow layers of human behavior and psychology. It's not enough to focus on the I in IT. We must also lose the C in HCI. Because ambient findability is less about the computer than the complex interactions between humans and information.

Findability is the biggest story on the Web today, and its reach will only grow as the tidal waves of channel convergence and ubiquitous computing wash over our shores. We will use the Web to navigate a physical world that sparkles with embedded sensors and geospatial metadata, even as we diminish the need to move our bodies through space. Mobile devices will unite our data streams in an evolving dance of informed consumers seeking collective intelligence and inspiration. And in this ambient economy, findability will be a key source of competitive advantage. Finders, keepers; losers, weepers.

Paradise Lost

Have you ever been to Lost and Found? It's a shadowy place we discover only through loss. It's filled with hats, mittens, watches, toys, and rings of gold and silver. And it smells of hope and fear and musty books. A child's first visit is a powerful experience. A valued possession has been lost. Perhaps in the classroom or on the playground. A frantic search leads to tearful resignation. Finders, keepers; losers, weepers.

---

* Inspired by the words of physics genius Richard Feynman, whose 1959 talk entitled "There's Plenty of Room at the Bottom" launched the field of nanotechnology.

But wait. A classmate steps forward. Have you tried the Lost and Found? Understanding is instant. A place for lost things. That makes sense. A short walk to an office with a cardboard box under a table. There it is. That's mine. A happy ending.

Of course, sometimes finders are keepers. Sometimes things get lost between the cracks. It depends what you lose and where and when. The idea of Lost and Found is universal. It's a social institution that transcends place and time. But the instantiation is another matter. A cardboard box in your local school. A steel cage in a foreign airport. The idea adapts to suit its environment. Each instance is defined by location.

Or at least it was until that disruptive technology known as the Internet came along. People from all over can now report and seek items using the Internet Lost and Found. The site sports an international database of pet and property listings, and the stories of success touch the heart and mind. An 83-year-old woman recovers a beloved heirloom necklace. A 10-year-old boy is reunited with his English Springer Spaniel. Dogs, cats, watches, wallets. Lost in the world. Found in cyberspace. Our digital networks locate physical objects. Keyword search isn't just for documents anymore. Technology has entered the shadow lands of Lost and Found, and we ain't seen nothin' yet.

Some speak of a coming techno-utopia, a magical era when all our problems will fade into the sunset. The end of poverty and starvation. No more sickness and disease. Global peace. Eternal life. In the words of Ernest Hemingway in *The Sun Also Rises*, isn't it pretty to think so? The human condition won't be untangled so easily, and technology is a double-edged sword. Arthur C. Clarke once said "any sufficiently advanced technology is indistinguishable from magic." His remark conjures both promise and peril.

We can be surprised and delighted by innovation. A vaccine for smallpox. A man on the moon. A computer through the eye of a needle. Sometimes anything seems possible, and yet it's not. Technology remains subject to the laws of physics and the gravity of economics. Unfortunately, false prophets abound, and today's technology is advanced enough that we have a hard time separating fact from fiction.

On the Web, these prophets claim that artificial intelligence will make it easy for us to find what we need, or better yet, for our digital agents and smart services to find us. Indeed, progress will come, but it won't come so easy. Information anxiety will intensify, and we'll spend more time, rather than less, searching for what we need.

These sober predictions derive not from the laws of physics but from the limits of language. For that's what we talk about when we talk about findability. While the Web's architecture rests on a solid foundation of code, its usefulness depends on the slippery slope of semantics. It's all about words. Words as labels. Words as links. Keywords.

And words are messy little critters. Imprecise and undependable, their meaning shifts with context. One man's paradise is another man's oblivion. Synonyms, antonyms, homonyms, contranyms: the challenges of communication are part of the human condition, unsusceptible to the eager advances of technology.

Some speak of a coming techno-dystopia, a brave new world of more ignorance and less freedom. Librarians worry about students who never step foot in libraries, a dot.net generation that goes to Google when they need to read. One woman I met at a conference in Paris even accused the Internet of creating "a black hole in our cultural heritage."

While sometimes funny, these fears aren't irrational or insignificant, but they don't keep me up at night. Because, when it comes to the Internet and the future of ambient findability, I'm an optimist. In Marshall McLuhan's insight that the medium is the message, I see the power of the Internet to engage people as participants in the collaborative, productive enterprise of knowledge creation and dissemination. For information is ultimately about communication. As S.I. Hayakawa once wrote:

> In addition to having developed language, human beings have also developed means of making, on clay tablets, bits of wood or stone, skins of animals, paper and microchips, more or less permanent marks and scratches that stand for language...Humans are no longer dependent for information upon direct experience alone. Instead of exploring the false trails others have explored and repeating their errors, they can go on from where others left off. Language makes progress possible.[*]

We take language and the Internet for granted, yet they are testaments to human ingenuity and our ability to enlist selfish genes in remarkable acts of cooperation. So, as the Web rolls on, I don't fear the loss of culture. On the contrary, the Web makes our cultural heritage more accessible. The dialogues of Plato, the sonnets of Shakespeare, and the poetry of *Paradise Lost* are all findable and accessible, even from a beach in Newport.

Yesterday will not be lost, and we won't find paradise in the morning. But tomorrow will be different. Findability is at the center of a quiet revolution in how we define authority, allocate trust, and make decisions. We won't forget the past, but we will reinvent the future. And as we wander into the uncharted territory between the land of atoms and the sea of bits, we should bring a compass, or even better, a Treo, because the journey transforms the destination, and it's easy to become lost in reflection.

---

[*] *Language in Thought and Action* by S.I. Hayakawa. Harcourt (1939), p. 6–7.

CHAPTER 2
A Brief History of Wayfinding

Not all those who wander are lost.
—J.R.R. Tolkien

Labyrinths and mazes are two distinct creatures. In the modern world, we are most familiar with the maze, an intricate and often confusing network of interconnecting pathways or tunnels designed to challenge the skills of all who enter. Mazes are multicursal. They offer a choice of paths, along with a disorienting mix of twists, turns, blind alleys, and dead ends. In a maze, it's hard to find your way and easy to become lost.

In contrast, a true labyrinth is unicursal, like the one in Figure 2-1. There is one well-defined path that leads into the center and back out again. The labyrinth is an ancient symbol with a 3,500 year history in religion and mythology in such diverse places as Egypt, Peru, Arizona, Iceland, India, and Sumatra. It combines the imagery of circle and spiral into a meandering but purposeful path, a reassuring metaphor for our journey through life.

In practice, we use the terms interchangeably. Our most famous labyrinth was really a maze, designed by the skillful architect Daedalus to entomb the Minotaur and its victims. Only by relying on Ariadne's ball of thread was Theseus able to escape after slaying the beast at the center. Like today's mazes of hedge and corn and ink, the labyrinth of Crete was a puzzle, inviting competitors to test their skills.

Semantics aside, our fascination with labyrinths and mazes stems from a primal fear of being lost. Over the course of history, the ability to venture out in search of food, water, and companionship, and then find our way home again has been central to survival. For animals and humans alike, getting lost has typically been a very dangerous prospect.

Our wayfinding instincts testify to the power of evolution. The diversity and sophistication of natural orientation and navigation skills is breathtaking.

Figure 2-1. A true labyrinth presents a single path to the center

The environment challenges and evolution responds. And, of course, humans have also responded by creating wayfinding tools and technologies and by shaping the very environments in which we live.

In fact, the term *wayfinding* originated in the context of what architects call the built environment. First used by architect Kevin Lynch in 1960 to describe the role of maps, street numbers, directional signs, and other "wayfinding" devices in cities, the term has since been appropriated by biologists, anthropologists, and psychologists to describe the behavior of animals and humans in natural and artificial environments.

A Definition of Wayfinding

Wayfinding is a fancy word for the series of things people know and do in order to get from one place to another, inside or outside. Wayfinding can be a snap or an onerous take, depending on the person, the environment, and the situation. You can think of wayfinding as a five step process. It starts with knowing where you are. It means knowing your destination, following the best route to your destination, being able to recognize your destination, and finding your way back to your starting point.

—*Directional Sense* by Jan Carpman and
Myron Grant. Evans & Co. (2006)

Most recently, wayfinding has been applied to the study of user behavior within digital information environments. We talk about people getting lost in cyberspace. We create "breadcrumbs" and "landmarks" to support orientation and navigation in web sites. While these spatial metaphors are often taken too far, there is no doubting their resonance.

We do import our natural wayfinding behaviors and vocabularies into digital environments, and for that reason alone, the history of wayfinding is worth our attention. But at the intersection of location awareness and ubiquitous computing, we are increasingly navigating hybrid environments that connect physical and digital. The history of wayfinding only grows more interesting with each step into the future.

All Creatures Great and Small

Before we lavish attention on Homo sapiens, it's worth taking a look at the wayfinding skills of a few other species with which we share planet Earth. Their solutions to the challenges of orientation and navigation can illuminate our own. For example, have you ever wondered how ants find a feeding site and then return home? Lacking maps and street signs and cell phones, these tiny creatures regularly travel thousands of times their own body length to arrive at a pinpoint goal.

After decades of research, behavioral biologists have begun to figure out how. Studies show that ants use a combination of geocentric and egocentric techniques. Geocentric navigation (also called allocentric or exocentric) relies on external environmental cues such as landmarks and any available map information. Ants make intensive use of visual landmarks. In effect, ants take snapshots as they proceed from one location to another, and they're able to rely on those visual memories to retrace their routes. Before leaving home, an ant takes a visual snapshot of the panorama as seen from the nest. Upon return, the ant finds its nest by positioning itself so the current image of the environment matches the stored snapshot. If the image is smaller than the snapshot, the ant moves closer. If the image is larger, the ant moves away. Research shows that ants make use of multiple, successive snapshots to find their way along each foraging route.

However, this use of visual landmarks is not sufficient. Some landmarks move. Others become blocked from view. In many environments, memorable features are hard to find. The Sahara desert, home to the *Cataglyphis* ants, is particularly hostile to landmark navigation. And that's where egocentric navigation comes in. Egocentric navigation relies on self-awareness of distance and direction traveled and is independent of the immediate surroundings. Ants employ an egocentric strategy known as path integration to retrace their steps. This strategy is made possible by two remarkable senses. First, ants possess the biological equivalent of an odometer that tells them not just how many steps they have taken but the ground-level distance traveled during each segment of the journey. Second, ants possess a skylight compass that relies on the position of the sun as indicated by polarized light to compute direction. By combining knowledge of distance and direction, ants have a basic ability to retrace their steps independent of landmarks. Of course, these senses are imperfect, and errors can rapidly accumulate during the course of a trip. It's the sophisticated combination of strategies that allows for error correction and ultimate wayfinding success.

Sight. Hearing. Touch. Smell. Taste. We're often intrigued by the novel application of these five senses. Bats and whales and dolphins use echolocation to "hear" their way through low visibility environments. Salmon rely on a powerful sense of smell to sniff out routes as they navigate back to the upstream waters where they will breed. A "signature scent" characterized by the chemical composition of rocks and minerals leads them back to their place of birth. We're also impressed by unfamiliar wayfinding senses such as the polarized vision of ants and honeybees or the biomagnetism of sea turtles, lobsters, and newts. We can't help but speculate what it would be like to possess these remarkable capabilities. No wonder extra senses are a hallmark of our comic superheroes.

However, the story grows more interesting when we look beyond the senses to solve the puzzles of complex wayfinding behavior. Edward C. Tolman, a famous behavioral psychologist best known for his studies of learning in rats using mazes, provided new insight into the mysteries of wayfinding in his 1948 paper entitled "Cognitive Maps in Rats and Men."[*] The experiments began with rats exploring mazes in search of food. Through a process of trial and error, the rats learned to avoid deadends and increasingly select the best path to success. Over time, error rates fell and completion times dropped. At this point, the researchers changed the game by blocking some routes and opening up new ones. In response, the rats demonstrated an impressive ability to navigate the modified maze. Tolman concluded that rats construct a representation of their environment that allows them to take novel paths when the learned path is blocked. He called this representation a "cognitive map," a concept that has since been used to explain a wide variety of wayfinding behavior.

Most recently, marine biologists at the University of North Carolina have uncovered an even more sophisticated use of cognitive maps. We have long suspected that baby sea turtles have a built-in compass to guide them during their first open ocean migration. But, with the help of a massive cube-shaped coil system that can be used to reproduce the magnetic fields of various locations along the coast, these researchers have found that older turtles

---

[*] "Cognitive Maps in Rats and Men" by Edward C. Tolman (1948). *The Psychological Review*, vol. 55, no. 4, p. 189–208.

develop a "magnetic map" that includes their position and direction relative to home. Their magnetic sense combines with a natural mapping capability to form the biological equivalent of a global positioning system.

Finally, any account of animal wayfinding would be incomplete without the dance of the honeybee. Back in 350 B.C., the Greek philosopher and scientist, Aristotle, wrote in *Historia Animalium* (the *History of Animals*), "Each bee on her return is followed by three or four companions…how they do it has not yet been observed." A couple of thousand years later, we have a pretty good idea how they do it. We know that like ants, bees employ a combination of egocentric and geocentric strategies including a well-developed odometer, polarized vision, and landmark navigation. Bees also use color, scent, and even taste to supplement their nectar finding abilities. But what's really amazing about honeybees is their use of symbolic language to communicate the distance, direction, and quality of a food source. Individual honeybees describe the location of food through an elaborate "tail-wagging" dance. The message is amplified when multiple individuals point their fellow hive members to the same source. Not only do bees use language to support group wayfinding behavior. They also participate in collaborative filtering. Not bad for a bunch of insects!

As Edward O. Wilson, the father of sociobiology, suggests in *The Future of Life*, we can learn a lot from the millions of species surrounding us. In the realm of medicine alone, we humans stand to benefit tremendously. Nine of the 10 leading prescription drugs originated from living organisms, and we've hardly begun to tap the world's store of biodiversity. In fact, we have yet to find or name the majority of species. Roughly 1.8 million species have been discovered, but estimates of the true number of living species range from 3.6 million to 100 million. That's a pretty wide range. If we've barely begun counting the species, imagine how much we have to learn by studying their behavior.

Human Wayfinding in Natural Habitats

What single characteristic distinguishes humans from all other animals? Our labels reflect attempts to answer this question. Homo habilis or "handy man" suggests the importance of tool use. Homo erectus or "upright man" emphasizes hands-free, heads-up, bipedal locomotion. And, Homo sapiens or "thinking man" invokes the value of intelligence and the capacity for language. In truth, we have much in common with our fellow creatures, including identical chunks of DNA and a common evolutionary heritage dating back four billion years. And for most of our history, we've wandered the same natural habitats without the benefit of compass, map, or signpost. It's no surprise that animals and humans share similar navigation skills and behaviors.

Unfortunately, we know very little about the two million year "prehistory" of human wayfinding. Prior to the invention of written language 5,500 years ago, we are left only with crumbling skulls and educated guesses. Our understanding flows primarily from modern studies in anthropology, archaeology, psychology, biology, and neuroscience. For example, it's a safe bet that early humans were dependent on the five basic senses. Though we talk about our "sense of direction," research has shown no convincing indication it exists. Lacking the polarized vision of ants and the magnetoreceptors of turtles, we have had to rely heavily on an awareness of our own movements (path integration) and a meticulous attention to environmental clues.

Today, much of this tacit knowledge, this ability to "read" the natural environment has been lost. Most of us can't set course by the position of the sun or the vegetation and moisture patterns on north and south facing slopes. Consequently, we underestimate the richness of available cues and marvel at the mysterious skills of our ancestors, such as the Polynesians who navigated open ocean voyages without instruments. In tiny canoes, they explored the vastness of the world's oceans, discovering such uninhabited and disparate islands as Samoa, Tonga, Tahiti, Hawaii, and New Zealand. Employing an ancient art of navigation, these seafaring explorers relied solely on careful observation of natural signs to reckon direction and location. The sun, moon, stars, and planets served as broad navigational framework. Ocean swells, winds, landmarks, and seamarks such as schools of fish, flocks of birds, and clusters of driftwood provided more localized clues.

Ethnographers often provide a glimpse into the past by studying indigenous, living societies that have preserved their ancient culture and tradition. In 1936, the anthropologist Raymond Firth wrote:

> The island of Tikopia is an example of another sort of system which is neither universal, egocentric, nor directed toward a base point, but is tied to a particular edge in the landscape. The island is small enough so that one is rarely out of sight or sound of the sea, and the islanders use the expressions inland or seaward for all kinds of spatial reference....Firth reports overhearing one man say to another: "There is a spot of mud on your seaward cheek."*

The use of prominent landmarks such as a mountain as the primary means of orientation has been observed in many societies, but only a very small island would support the particular system employed by the Tikopians.

---

* Quoted in *The Image of the City* by Kevin Lynch. MIT Press (1960), p. 129.

Unique environments produce unique solutions. And since necessity is the mother of invention, harsh environments produce creative solutions. Nowhere is this more evident than in the Songlines of the Aboriginal Australians. For thousands of years, these people navigated their rough and unforgiving land by inventing, memorizing and following an intricate series of songs that identified critical paths and landmarks. These oral road maps told how the features of the desert landscape were formed and named during the period of creation known as the Dreamtime. These songs were cultural and spiritual treasures. They also led you to the next waterhole.

> What did the first signs look like? Broken branches on the hunting paths of prehistoric man? Piles of rocks guiding nomadic tribes to their next camp? Maybe even earlier than that—claw marks on tree bark, or scent messages, the keys for which have been lost long ago.
>
> —Romedi Passini

Of course, while most people were doing things the hard way, early "handy man" geeks were learning to hack the environment. The earliest examples were most likely real, physical hacks: marks on bark indicating a path through the woods. Why rely on natural landmarks when you can create your own? Just don't use breadcrumbs. As Hansel and Gretel would testify, the birds will eat them. Speaking of hungry birds, Norwegian seafaring hackers learned to bring ravens on long voyages. When they thought land was near, the sailors released the birds, which had been deliberately starved. The ravenous ravens often headed "as the crow flies" directly toward land.

Most of the written history of wayfinding concerns the invention or adaptation of tools to support nautical exploration. The limited availability of landmarks and seamarks combined with the high cost of getting lost to provide a powerful incentive to be inventive. Consider the following solutions employed by sailors over the centuries:

Lighthouse
> The earliest recorded lighthouses were bonfires. They served as highly visible landmarks for sailors. The lighthouse of Alexandria, built around 270 B.C., was named one of the seven wonders of the ancient world. A mirror reflected sunlight during the day and a fire guided sailors at night. At 400 feet, it was among the tallest manmade structures on earth.

Compass

The Chinese used a magnetic device for land navigation called a "point-south carriage" as early as the third millennium B.C. In the West, the first mention of a compass comes in 1187 when englishman Alexander Neckham writes that "sailors use a magnetic needle which swings on a point and shows the direction of the north when the weather is overcast." Early compasses were very crude. A navigator would rub an iron needle against a piece of magnetic iron ore known as a "lodestone." He'd then place the needle in a piece of straw and float it in a bowl of water where it would point to the magnetic north pole. Many sailors believed the compass operated by black magic. Thanks to superstition and the inaccuracy caused by magnetic variation, the compass was not widely used until the 1700s.

Chip log

Over the years, sailors used a variety of dead-reckoning methods to compute distance traveled at sea. One method involved the use of an 18 inch chip of wood tied to a long rope with knots every 47 feet 3 inches. The chip was thrown over the stern (back end), and the number of knots were counted as they passed overboard until an hourglass filled with 30 seconds worth of sand had expired. The faster the ship was sailing, the more knots played out. Five knots was equivalent to five nautical miles per hour. We still refer to miles per hour on the water as "knots."

Sextant

Preceded by the Arabian kamal and the medieval astrolabe, the sextant constituted a breakthrough in global positioning, enabling sailors to compute their latitude (north-south position) to within a nautical mile or two by measuring the angle of heavenly bodies (i.e., sun, moon, planets, stars) above a horizontal line of reference, and then consulting an almanac prepared by astronomers that forecast the position of those heavenly bodies hour by hour many years into the future.

Chronometer

To determine longitude (east-west position) with sufficient precision, it became evident that a more accurate time-keeping device was needed. Sailors knew that for every 15 degrees traveled eastward, the local time moves ahead one hour. So, if they knew the time at two points on earth, they could calculate longitude based on the difference between them. They could measure the local time by observing the sun, but the trick was keeping track of time at a reference point such as Greenwich, England (the prime meridian). Pendulum clocks didn't work well at sea. Solving this problem was considered so important that countries began to offer prizes. In 1764, John Harrison won the British prize by inventing a seagoing chronometer accurate to one-tenth of a second per day. A few years later, Captain James Cook used Harrison's chronometer to circumnavigate the globe.

Maps and Charts

From the lighthouse to the chronometer, our inventors kept at it until we could compute distance, direction, and position from anywhere in the world. Of course, most of these wayfinding devices would have been relatively useless without the remarkable invention we know as the map. Though the oldest existing maps are preserved on Babylonian clay tablets from 2500 B.C., shown in Figure 2-2, the first maps were undoubtedly created thousands of years before in early hunter-gatherer societies, where crude diagrams sketched in the dirt were used to show paths and destinations within a local area. This ability to transform "cognitive maps" gained from personal experience into symbolic visual representations provided humans with a powerful cooperative advantage. Maps enabled us to share wayfinding experiences and geographic knowledge, thereby extending our communal ability to explore wider and wider regions without becoming afraid or getting lost. We could tell each other where to find food and we could warn of dangers to avoid.

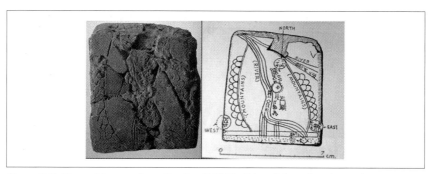

Figure 2-2. Clay tablet map from Ga-Sur (2500 B.C.) on left; redrawing with interpretation on right (images from http://www.henry-davis.com/MAPS/AncientWebPages/100D.html)

For many centuries, maps and mapmakers played a powerful role in defining the elements and edges of the known world. As Alfred Korzybksi, the father of general semantics, famously remarked: "the map is not the territory." No map can depict every physical feature of even the smallest area. All maps are estimations, generalizations, and interpretations. Maps are not so much about attention to detail as the selection of detail (Figure 2-3). Mapmakers choose which landmarks and paths to show and which to hide, and they decide where to draw the boundaries. On some maps, like the one in Figure 2-2, those boundaries marked the limits of one's territory: to venture outside the lines was to enter a no man's land between tribes. On other maps, those boundaries marked the edge of the world, literally (Figure 2-4). For much of antiquity people believed in a flat earth and feared falling off the edge. Maps reflect and shape the beliefs of a community or civilization. Beyond this place, there be dragons!

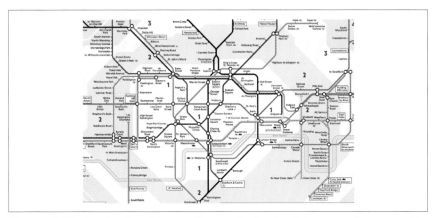

Figure 2-3. The London Tube Map sacrifices reality for simplicity, presenting memorable paths, edges, districts, nodes, and landmarks (image from http://www.tfl.gov.uk/tube/ maps)

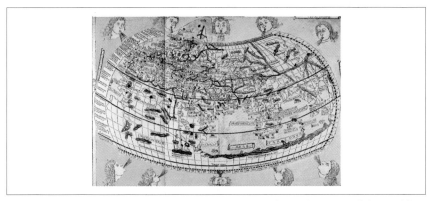

Figure 2-4. Ptolemy's map of the world, circa 150 A.D. (from The Image of the World [Whitfield, 1994]; available at http://academic.emporia.edu/aberjame/map/h_map/ h_map.htm)

The refutation of the flat earth theory clearly had major political, religious, cultural, and commercial implications. Proposed by Pythagoras in 500 B.C. and proved by Aristotle in 350 B.C., the round earth theory set the stage for global exploration, international trade, and modern mapmaking. Early maps of the known world were hand drawn. Consequently, they were very rare and very expensive. The invention of the printing press made maps more widely available, thereby sparking the Age of Exploration in the 15th and 16th centuries. Extensive travel and careful observation led to more detailed maps and navigation charts with coast lines, islands, rivers, and safe harbors. The military and economic value of these maps did not go unnoticed: many were designated as classified national or commercial secrets.

In 1569, Gerardus Mercator of Belgium published a map of the world based on a cylindrical projection that allowed for easier and more accurate navigation of a round world via a flat map. To achieve this goal, the Mercator Projection distorted the true layout of the Earth, exaggerating the size of areas far from the equator. Greenland looked equivalent in size to Africa, which is actually 13 times bigger. Europe appeared in the center and larger than life, a feature that contributed to the map's early popularity. But most importantly, the projection worked. It's still widely used today, though it's accused of perpetuating the perceived inferiority of the "Third World."

Despite the prevalence of national mapping programs, much of the Earth was uncharted until the widespread use of aerial photography following World War II. Advances in the use of radio signal–based navigation and positioning systems such as radar and Loran in the 1930s and 1940s dramatically increased the efficiency and precision of these mapping efforts. In the 1970s, we began pouring all this spatial data into geographic information systems (GIS). Traditionally, the map served as both database and display. GIS established the separation of the data and presentation layers, allowing for many of today's mobile, network-enabled navigation devices. Of course, today we're more likely to use our maps and GPS systems to navigate the streets of an unfamiliar city than the Straits of Gibraltar. Our everyday experiences with wayfinding are based largely in surroundings of our own making. This brings us, quite naturally, to the built environment.

The Built Environment

In his 1960 book, *The Image of the City*, Kevin Lynch inspired a generation of architects, planners, designers, and citizens to envision urban spaces as a functioning whole. Using the concept of environmental *legibility*, he focused attention on the structure and organization of a city's wayfinding systems. Drawing upon extensive studies conducted in Boston, Jersey City, and Los

Angeles, Lynch brought to life the orientation and navigation experiences of real people in real cities. He contrasted the anxiety and even terror caused by disorientation with the sense of balance and well-being produced by the easily recognizable patterns of a legible city. And he created a vocabulary for describing a city's elements that laid the foundation for modern wayfinding design.

Paths
> The streets, walkways, transit lines, canals, railroads, and other channels through which people occasionally or regularly move.

Edges
> The walls, shores, fences, barriers, and other boundaries that create linear breaks in continuity, both separating and relating two distinct regions.

Districts
> Major sections of the city that possess a common identifying character (e.g., The Financial District, The North End, China Town).

Nodes
> Intersections, enclosed squares, street corners, subway stations, and other transportation hubs that serve as points of reference, transition, and destination.

Landmarks
> Towering buildings, golden domes, mountains, signs, storefronts, trees, doorknobs, and other physical objects that serve as spatial reference points.

People construct an environmental image of the city, composed of these building blocks, that provides context and supports wayfinding. In the shadow of the Eiffel Tower, the straight *path* of the Avenue des Champs Elysées, shown in Figure 2-5, connects the *landmarks* of the Arc de Triomphe and the Louvre, creating one of many powerful combinations that makes Paris a legible city. In contrast, Boston's winding streets and dearth of high-visibility landmarks (not to mention the perpetual construction project known as the Big Dig) combine to disorient travelers, making them need maps like that in Figure 2-6. As Lynch's title suggests, the impact of legibility goes beyond wayfinding; it shapes people's image of the city. Getting lost in a city can be frustrating and scary. Frequent negative experiences hurt the city's brand. In contrast, landmarks that combine form and function by serving as beautiful wayfinding tools can greatly enhance the city's image. San Francisco's Golden Gate Bridge (Figure 2-7) and Turin's Mole Antonelliana (Figure 2-8) are just a couple of widely admired examples.

Figure 2-5. Avenue des Champs Elysées in Paris

Following in the footsteps of Kevin Lynch, designer Paul Arthur and architect Romedi Passini advanced our understanding of the built environment in their 1992 book, *Wayfinding: People, Signs, and Architecture*. In this landmark text, the authors make the economic and ethical case for the importance of wayfinding design:

> The trouble is that we don't care enough about wayfinding (let alone signs) to insist on doing the job properly.
>
> Many buildings have no numbers on them, and when they do, there is no concern for their legibility. In the hours of darkness all this becomes even worse because very few street signs are ever illuminated. The only signs that are routinely illuminated in North America are billboards and traffic signals.
>
> In a medium-sized hospital up to 8000 hours a year of staff time (or four person-years) are spent explaining the signs and redirecting people...The single thing the public most dreads about hospitals and health-care facilities is getting lost in them.
>
> Architects and graphic designers have tended to see the user of their settings as a stereotyped, physically fit, attentive individual, with only one preoccupation—to explore and enjoy the settings they have created. The reality,

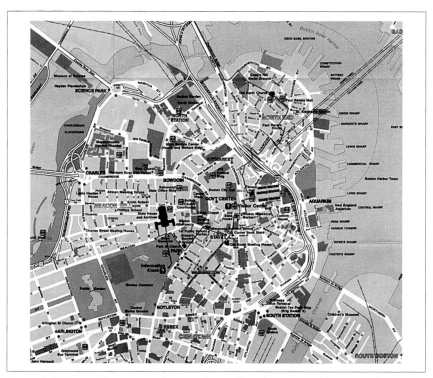

Figure 2-6. The winding streets of Boston (image from http://www.lib.utexas.edu/maps/ national_parks/boston_map.jpg)

however, is quite different. Many users have impairments in respect to perception, cognition, and mobility (physical behavior) which affect their wayfinding abilities.[*]

Arthur and Passini remind us that poor wayfinding design (see Figure 2-9) doesn't just lead to frustration, wasted time, and missed connections in airports and train stations. People die because ambulance drivers can't find their way to an address in time. People die because of badly placed or poorly labeled fire exits. People die because they're looking at a map instead of the road. Because of poor wayfinding design, people die. And the significant (and growing) numbers of people with disabilities from those with limited vision to those suffering from Alzheimer's face greater wayfinding challenges and risks than most.

---

[*] *Wayfinding: People, Signs, and Architecture* by Paul Arthur and Romedi Passini. McGraw-Hill Ryerson (1992).

Figure 2-7. San Francisco's Golden Gate Bridge serves as path, landmark, node, and edge

Having illustrated the problems of wayfinding, the authors explain how architects, urban planners, graphic designers, and building managers can create solutions:

> We always provide information in sequence. Information about the destination zones appears once the visitors have entered the buildings.
>
> On signs and maps, only a small number of written items, generally three at most, can be read at a glance.
>
> Subway route maps have been effective because of, and not despite, the way in which they have sacrificed reality for simplicity.
>
> Finally, we reiterate the importance of redundancy in wayfinding communication. The use of multiple means to communicate the same information is the best guarantee that the message gets across.[*]

It's interesting to consider the applicability of these recommendations to online information systems. The lessons from the built environment fit nicely with the exhortations of web usability experts such as Jakob Nielsen and Steve Krug. Users don't read, they scan. Break up pages into clearly defined areas. Provide multiple navigational paths. Keep it simple. Don't make me think!

---

[*] Arthur and Passini (1992).

Figure 2-8. La Mole Antonelliana is a landmark in the heart of Turin; as a museum for the history of cinema, it's also a favored destination

Figure 2-9. All of us have been confused by signage

Of course, there are fundamental differences between physical and digital realms, and we'll get to those soon. But for now, let's conclude our focus on the built environment by acknowledging a theme that courses through the literature of wayfinding and usability alike: the vital importance of *empathy* for the user. Only by understanding and caring about the perspective of the individual can we design useful, usable solutions. Only by designing for emergent patterns of use that flow from common needs, desires, instincts, and behaviors can we create shared spaces that unite form and function.

As the architect Christopher Alexander asserts:

> There is one timeless way of building. It is thousands of years old, and the same today as it has always been. The great traditional buildings of the past, the villages and tents and temples in which man feels at home, have always been made by people who were very close to the center of this way. It is not possible to make great buildings, or great towns, beautiful places, places where you feel yourself, places where you feel alive, except by following this way. And...this way will lead anyone who looks for it to buildings which are themselves as ancient in their form, as the trees and hills, and as our faces are.[*]

From the hunter-gatherers of the African Savannah to the commuters of New York and Los Angeles to the searchers of Yahoo! and Google, humans have drawn upon an inherited set of senses and skills to navigate dissimilar environments. Our surroundings change, but the wheels of evolution turn slow. As the information age propels us faster and deeper into cyberspace, an appreciation for the history of wayfinding behavior in natural and built environments will prove quite handy.

Wayfinding in the Noosphere

Have you heard of the hippocampus? It's one of the most ancient parts of the brain, located deep within the temporal lobes and adjacent to the amygdala. This horseshoe-shaped structure plays a central role in learning, memory, and wayfinding. We know rats rely on the hippocampus for maze navigation. It's essential for both path integration and the processing of cognitive maps. We know neurons called "place cells" are intensely active when a rat revisits familiar locations. And we know animals and humans experience severe disorientation when the hippocampus is damaged.

Magnetic resonance imaging (MRI) scans have shown an enlarged posterior region of the hippocampus in taxi drivers, and Positron Emission Tomography (PET) scans show increased hippocampal activity when drivers are asked to recall routes around the city. In recent years, researchers have conducted similar experiments in virtual environments. Sure enough, when subjects are exploring a virtual maze or the artificial terrain of a video game, those same neurons light up. Does this constitute evidence of a biological basis for the validity of wayfinding metaphors on the World Wide Web? Not quite. Virtual mazes and semantic spaces are not equivalent. But it does remind us that when we enter the artificial noosphere, we bring our natural instincts and our physical bodies with us.

---

[*] *The Timeless Way of Building* by Christopher Alexander. Oxford University Press (1979), p. 7.

A Jesuit paleontologist and philosopher by the name of Teilhard de Chardin popularized the notion of the noosphere or "sphere of human thought" back in the early 1900s. Similar to the atmosphere and biosphere, the noosphere is composed of all the interacting minds and ideas on earth. It's a provocative and romantic concept. But is the noosphere real? Or is it just a metaphor, a figure of speech for relating our experience of the physical world to the ethereal realm of knowledge?

Well, there's a distinguished linguistics professor at UC Berkeley who would take issue with its dismissal as *just* a metaphor. George Lakoff has spent many years researching the subtle power of metaphor to interpret and shape our experience. In the book *Metaphors We Live By*, he and his co-author explain:

> Metaphor is pervasive in everyday life, not just in language but in thought and action….The concepts that govern our thought are not just matters of the intellect. They also govern our everyday functioning, down to the most mundane details. Our concepts structure what we perceive, how we get around in the world, and how we relate to other people…the way we think, what we experience, and what we do every day is very much a matter of metaphor.[*]

Interestingly, Lakoff and Johnson dedicate a chapter to orientational metaphors that are mostly spatial in nature: up-down, in-out, front-back, on-off, deep-shallow, and central-peripheral. These metaphors "arise from the fact that we have bodies of the sort we have and that they function as they do in our physical environment." For each metaphor type, the authors suggest a physical basis. For example:

HAPPY IS UP; SAD IS DOWN

> I'm feeling *up*. That *boosted* my spirits. My spirits *rose*. You're in *high* spirits. Thinking about her always gives me a *lift*. I'm feeling *down*. I'm *depressed*. He's really *low* these days. I *fell* into a depression. My spirits *sank*.

> Physical basis: Drooping posture typically goes along with sadness and depression, erect posture with a positive emotional state.[†]

Spatial and orientational metaphors have deep roots in our physical experience, and yet they're forever sprouting in the unearthly terrain of the noosphere. Readers get *lost* in a good book. Lawyers review *landmark* cases. Users *navigate* web sites. We use language to construct worlds of words that are, in a very real sense, navigable. While today's attention is focused on the semantic cities of cyberspace and the Web, language and wayfinding have walked hand in hand from the beginning. In fact, evidence points to the

---

[*] *Metaphors We Live By*. George Lakoff and Mark Johnson. University of Chicago Press (1980), p. 3.
[†] Lakoff and Johnson, p. 15.

gestural origins of language around 500,000 years ago. It's likely that our first words were actually vocalized grunts and squeals used to draw attention to manual gestures indicating the direction of food, water, home, or danger. Look! Over there! Watch out!

Over time, we developed a sophisticated vocabulary for describing routes, landmarks, and destinations. The Songlines of Australia and the *Odyssey* of Homer stand testament to the interwoven histories of oral communication and wayfinding. For many millennia, we used words to cooperatively navigate physical spaces, and then, in an interesting metaphorical twist, we began using the concept of space to organize our ideas:

> Two thousand years ago Marcus Tullius Cicero used to make two-hour speeches in the Roman Senate, without notes, by constructing in his mind a palace whose rooms and furnishings, as he imagined himself roaming through them, called up the ideas he wished to discuss: ideas were made memorable by locating them in space.[*]

Of course, this mastery of the memory palace was limited to the few. It took the printed word, the proliferation of talking objects called documents, and the invention of libraries for these spatial metaphors to flourish. Suddenly, people found themselves literally surrounded by ideas. Imagine standing in the Library of Alexandria in 150 B.C. The walls are lined with tens of thousands of scrolls containing the best thoughts of the best minds in the world. To find the knowledge you seek, you must rely on bibliographies, subject catalogs, and other finding aids. And you must move through physical space to locate and retrieve information objects. How could you fail to perceive this experience in terms of navigation and wayfinding? Libraries exist at the very intersection of physical and semantic space. They inform and inspire our sense of the noosphere.

So, it's no surprise the library made an appearance in Vannevar Bush's classic 1945 essay "As We May Think," which described collaborative hypertext for the first time:

> Consider a future device for individual use, which is a sort of mechanized private file and *library*. It needs a name, and to coin one at random, 'memex' will do. A memex is a device in which an individual stores all his books, records, and communications, and which is mechanized so that it may be consulted with exceeding speed and flexibility. It is an enlarged intimate supplement to his memory.
>
> The owner of the memex, let us say, is interested in the origin and properties of the bow and arrow. Specifically he is studying why the short Turkish bow was apparently superior to the English long bow in the skirmishes of the

---

[*] *Chambers for a Memory Palace* by Donlyn Lyndon and Charles W. Moore. MIT Press (1994), p. xi.

Crusades. He has dozens of possibly pertinent books and articles in his memex. First he runs through an encyclopedia, finds an interesting but sketchy article, leaves it projected. Next, in a history, he finds another pertinent item, and ties the two together.

Thus he goes, building a trail of many items. Occasionally he inserts a comment of his own, either linking it into the main trail or joining it by a side trail to a particular item. When it becomes evident that the elastic properties of available materials had a great deal to do with the bow, he branches off on a side trail which takes him through textbooks on elasticity and tables of physical constants. He inserts a page of longhand analysis of his own. Thus he builds a trail of his interest through the maze of materials available to him.

And his trails do not fade.[*]

While Bush's theoretical memex is widely considered a harbinger of today's World Wide Web, it was later in the 20th century, 1984 to be exact, when science-fiction author William Gibson lit up the imaginations of people around the world with his dystopic vision of a computer-generated parallel universe:

> Cyberspace. A consensual hallucination experienced daily by billions of legitimate operators, in every nation, by children being taught mathematical concepts....A graphic representation of data abstracted from the banks of every computer in the human system. Unthinkable complexity. Lines of light ranged in the nonspace of the mind, clusters and constellations of data. Like city lights, receding...[†]

In particular, Gibson's vision electrified a generation raised on rapidly evolving personal computers and video games. From the textual fantasies of Zork (Example 2-1) to the rich, immersive environments of Ultima, SimCity (Figure 2-10), Habitat, Myst (Figure 2-11), Doom, and Second Life (Figure 2-12), we had stepped through the looking glass of our computer monitor into worlds of adventure and beauty.

Example 2-1. Transcript from Zork, one of the first and most famous interactive fiction games

```
> EAST
The Troll Room
You are in a small room with passages off in all directions.
Bloodstains and deep scratches (perhaps made by an axe) mar the walls.
A nasty-looking troll, brandishing a bloody axe, blocks all passages out of the
room.
Your sword has begun to glow very brightly.
```

[*] "As We May Think" by Vannevar Bush. *The Atlantic Monthly* (1945).

[†] *Neuromancer* by William Gibson. The Berkeley Publishing Group (1984), p. 51.

Figure 2-10. In SimCity, you navigate a terrain of your own design

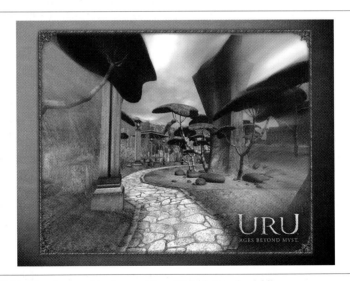

Figure 2-11. Myst is arguably the most beautiful of virtual worlds

Figure 2-12. Second Life is a 3D digital world created and populated by its networked residents

We faced the challenges of wayfinding in virtual worlds, learning to count steps, track direction, remember landmarks, and draw our own maps. We experienced Moore's law as a rapid progression from text-based interactive stories to immersive environments with rich graphics. We became excited by the potential of virtual reality and the Internet to breathe life into Gibson's cyberspace. We felt the future was just around the corner. And so naturally, when NCSA released the first graphical browser in 1993, we brought our enthusiasm, our vision, and our spatial metaphors to the World Wide Web.

The Web

The principles of wayfinding are clearly relevant in immersive virtual environments, from video games to architectural walkthroughs to battlefield simulations. But do they apply to the everyday Web? Does our knowledge of orientation and navigation in the physical world have value in the digital worlds of web sites and intranets? We've certainly created a multitude of spatial metaphors to explain the Web, from Al Gore's information superhighway to the proliferation of home pages, site maps, and breadcrumbs. And web designers have aggressively embraced metaphor by creating information architectures, blueprints, and navigation systems.

And yet, some researchers have begun to question the usefulness of these metaphors. Andrew Dillon and Misha Vaughan assert that "navigation is a limited metaphor for hypermedia and website use that potentially constrains our understanding of human-computer interaction." They argue that unlike physical navigation where the destination is the goal, in semantic spaces, the journey is the destination. They suggest, as an alternative, the concept of information shape and the harnessing of perceptual cues embedded in genre. As we'll discuss later, there is real potential in these ideas. The exploration of new metaphors and the courage to design beyond metaphor are both critical to innovation in web design. However, the positioning of shape and genre as replacing rather than complementing the navigation metaphor is a mistake. All metaphors have limits. All metaphors can be taken too far. But that does not negate their core value.

There is no question that people experience the Web as a type of space in which they move. A paper called "Metaphors We Surf the Web By" presents detailed evidence that web users remember and talk about the Web in terms of spatial navigation.[*] We use a mix of *trajectory* metaphors (e.g., "I went to the IBM home page") and *container* metaphors (e.g., "I found that inside Yahoo!"). We construct cognitive maps. We remember (and bookmark) landmarks and anchor points. We traverse paths or clickstreams in search of information objects. And we often become lost and disoriented.

On the other hand, attempts to map the Web using information visualization techniques mostly fail. Over the past decade, there have been a number of well-financed efforts to solve search and navigation problems with interactive maps. These companies and their products, shown in Figures 2-13 to 2-15, enjoy tons of media coverage because their pretty pictures and futuristic visions attract attention. They are held up as a revolutionary step forward in human-computer interaction. They are the Next Big Thing. And then they disappear.

These spatial visualization approaches fail because there's no there there. As David Weinberger explains, "The Web is a public place completely devoid of space....We can move from place to place but without having to traverse distance."[†] There are billions of web sites, and they're all a single click from each other. We do experience movement through sites. We can even rely on egocentric dead-reckoning techniques for wayfinding by recalling, for instance, that it was two clicks deep into the product taxonomy before the whitepaper link appeared. But that distance is not real. There's always a shortcut. There's always another route. A keyword search sorts through four billion pages in a quarter second. Google requires no metaphor. Just results. Text and hypertext. Fast. While the Web celebrates hypermedia, it is first and foremost a textual medium for communication and information sharing. Our experience of the Web depends upon the use of words to convey

---

[*] "Metaphors We Surf the Web By" by Paul P. Maglio and Teenie Matlock. Available at *http://www.almaden.ibm.com/cs/people/pmaglio/pubs/meta4surf.pdf*.

[†] *Small Pieces Loosely Joined* by David Weinberger. Perseus Publishing (2002), p. 50.

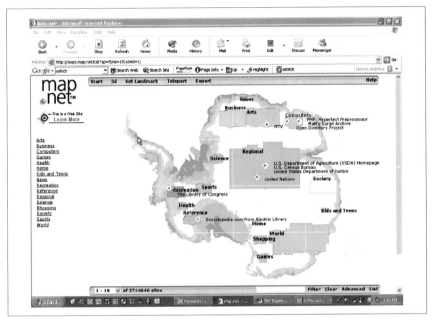

Figure 2-13. Antarcti.ca promised to improve web search and retrieval through visualization; though well-funded, much-hyped, and run by smart people, it failed to deliver a useful product

meaning. Words as labels. Words as links. Keywords. And though it's possible to communicate topical similarity visually as semantic distance, the image adds little to the text.

So, our spatial metaphors have limits. We can take them too far. And yet, they have real value and resonance. People do navigate web sites. Wayfinding does belong on the Web. But, there are complementary metaphors such as shape and genre that provide new inspiration for design. And sometimes, it's best to move beyond metaphor in search of innovation. It is for all these reasons that the Web deserves a word with one foot in the past and one in the future. This word *findability* draws upon our long heritage of wayfinding in natural and built environments, while invoking the practical, web-savvy focus of usability. Findability is a bridge that spans the physical and digital worlds, enabling us to import and export concepts at will. We shall be spending a great deal of time on this bridge as these worlds become increasingly intertwined.

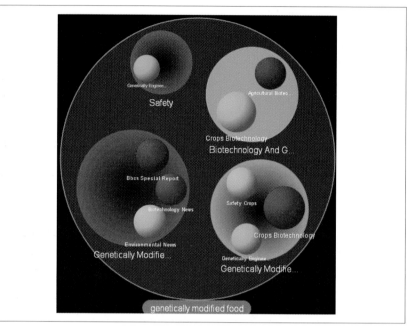

Figure 2-14. Grokker, a software product from Groxis, presents web search results visually in automatically generated categories; it's interesting and fun to play with, but it's not useful

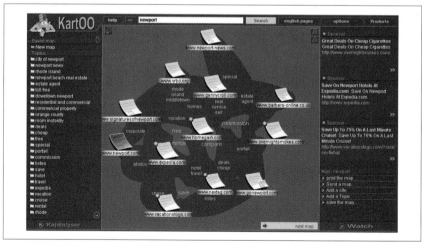

Figure 2-15. Kartoo presents web search results as a map

The Baldwin Effect

At the dawn of the 20th century, James Mark Baldwin, a pioneering developmental psychologist, began a line of inquiry into the coevolution of genes and culture that continues to this day. Baldwin asserted that organisms could survive ecological challenges by relying on acquired knowledge and skills, often learned from others, and that this may then channel natural selection to favor unlearned versions of the same behavior. This mechanism, now known as the Baldwin effect, suggests that organisms can learn to shape their environment and consequently alter the path of evolution. For example, we know dairy farming emerged before the spread of lactose absorption genes and created the selection pressures that favored them, not the other way around.

For those of us living in the modified ecologies of the 21st century, the Baldwin effect has special meaning. As a species, we have transformed our environment beyond recognition. We cannot help but wonder about the role and rules of natural selection in a society where the average life expectancy exceeds 75 years. And we must constantly struggle to reconcile our ancient survival instincts with modern reality. Behaviors that once kept us from starvation and predators now lead us into stress, obesity, and drug addiction. Evolution cannot keep pace with the environment. We must rely heavily on our intelligence, the gift of language, and our ability to learn and unlearn. For the proving grounds have shifted from natural and built environments to the noosphere, a world defined by symbols and semantics, a world that in certain respects does not exist, as Figure 2-16 reminds us.

Figure 2-16. René Magritte's assertion that "This is not a pipe" invites us to question the distinction between image and reality (© 2005 C. Herscovici, Brussels/Artists Rights Society [ARS], New York)

When pondering the reality of the noosphere or the substance of cyber-space, it's worth throwing memes into the mix. Richard Dawkins, one of the world's most prominent biologists, describes memes as follows:

> Examples of memes are tunes, ideas, catch-phrases, clothes' fashions, ways of making pots or of building arches. Just as genes propagate themselves in the gene pool by leaping from body to body via sperms or eggs, so memes propagate themselves in the meme pool by leaping from brain to brain via a process which, in the broad sense, can be called imitation. If a scientist hears, or reads about, a good idea, he passes it on to his colleagues and students. He mentions it in his articles and his lectures. If the idea catches on, it can be said to propagate itself, spreading from brain to brain. As my colleague N.K. Humphrey neatly summed up an earlier draft of this chapter: '…memes should be regarded as living structures, not just metaphorically but techni-cally.'(3) When you plant a fertile meme in my mind you literally parasitize my brain, turning it into a vehicle for the meme's propagation in just the way that a virus may parasitize the genetic mechanism of a host cell. And this isn't just a way of talking—the meme for, say, "belief in life after death" is actually realized physically, millions of times over, as a structure in the ner-vous systems of individual men the world over.[*]

When we talk about navigating the noosphere or wayfinding on the Web, we are not *just* using metaphor. The worlds of words and ideas are in a very real sense, real. When we enter these spaces, we bring our senses along for the ride. We rely on geocentric and egocentric strategies that have served us for millennia. We become disoriented. We get lost. We find our way. We learn. Our virtual experiences change us physically. Winston Churchill once remarked "We shape our buildings; thereafter they shape us." These words take on new meaning as our physical and digital structures and our every-day experiences become deeply and irrevocably interconnected.

> Like Shangri-la, like mathematics, like every story ever told or sung, a mental geography of sorts has existed in the living mind of every culture, a collective memory or hallucination, an agreed-upon territory of mythical figures, sym-bols, rules, and truths, owned and traversable by all who learned its ways, and yet free of the bounds of physical space and time.
>
> —Michael Benedikt, architect and author of *Cyberspace*, 1991

[*] *The Selfish Meme* by Richard Dawkins. Oxford University Press (1976), p.192.

CHAPTER 3

Information Interaction

Documents are, quite simply, talking things.
They are bits of the material world—clay,
stone, animal skin, plant fiber, sand—that
we've imbued with the ability to speak.
—David M. Levy
University of Washington iSchool

Let me tell you a story about the laws of Moore and Mooers. Once upon a time, in 1965 to be precise, an engineer named Gordon Moore boldly predicted the number of transistors per square inch on integrated circuits would double every year. In his landmark paper for the journal of *Electronics*, Moore conjectured:

> Integrated circuits will lead to such wonders as home computers—or at least terminals connected to a central computer—automatic controls for automobiles, and personal portable communications equipment. The electronic wristwatch needs only a display to be feasible today.[*]

Though his specific prediction was a bit optimistic—transistor density has doubled roughly every two years—his overall vision has played out remarkably well. The number of transistors per circuit grew from 50 in 1965 to 410 million in 2003 and is fast approaching 1 billion. In the four decades since his paper was published, Gordon founded and grew a rather successful company called Intel; home computers, the Internet, mobile computing (and electronic wristwatches) became reality; and Moore's Law attained mythic status. Its exponential growth curve has been a favorite prop among techno-evangelists for implying the imminent arrival of virtual reality, artificial intelligence, and the paperless society. Faster is better, they argue—more is more.

---

[*] "Cramming More Components onto Integrated Circuits" by Gordon E. Moore (1965). *Electronics*, vol. 38, no. 8.

This brings us to the second law, first formulated by Calvin Mooers in 1959.

> An information retrieval system will tend *not* to be used whenever it is more painful and troublesome for a customer to have information than for him not to have it.*

Sometimes we don't want new information, he argued—less is more. Now, Calvin Mooers was also a computer pioneer and entrepreneur. He coined the terms "information retrieval" and "descriptors," wrote some of the earliest interactive programming languages, and founded the Zator company to develop and market his ingenious automatic punch card information retrieval system. But despite his significant contributions, Mooers is little known outside the information science community, and neither is his law.

Even within this small community, Mooers' Law is often misinterpreted as a maxim about the importance of information system *usability*. In the words of online information industry pioneer and Dialog founder, Roger Summit, "Mooers' Law tells us that information will be used in direct proportion to how easy it is to obtain."† Though this insight is accurate and important, it's not what Calvin Mooers had in mind. Consider the author's explanation of his own law:

> It is now my suggestion that many people may not want information, and that they will avoid using a system precisely because it gives them information....Having information is painful and troublesome. We have all experienced this. If you have information, you must first read it, which is not always easy. You must then try to understand it....Understanding the information may show that your work was wrong, or may show that your work was needless....Thus not having and not using information can often lead to less trouble and pain than having and using it.‡

Unfortunately, nobody pays much attention to Calvin Mooers these days. And yet, Mooers' Law only becomes more relevant with every advance of Moore's Law. Fast, cheap processors powered a personal computer revolution and enabled the information explosion we call the Internet. Five exabytes of information. Half a million new libraries the size of the Library of Congress. That's how much new information we create in a year—92% of it stored on magnetic media.§ It's time we shifted our focus from creating

---

* Remarks by Calvin N. Mooers during a panel discussion at the Annual Meeting of the American Documentation Institute, October 24, 1959.

† "Mooers' Law: In and Out of Context" by Brice Austin. *Journal of the American Society for Information Science and Technology*, June 2001.

‡ Remarks by Calvin N. Mooers on October 24, 1959. Reprinted in the *Bulletin of the American Society for Information Science*, October/November 1996.

§ "How Much Information" by Peter Lyman and Hal R. Varian (2003). From *http://www.sims. berkeley.edu/how-much-info-2003*.

a wealth of information to addressing the ensuing poverty of attention. Because Moore's law doesn't apply to the human brain. In fact, we haven't upgraded our wetware much in the past 50,000 years.* Technology moves fast. Evolution moves slow. In recent years, the friction between these layers has given birth to usability, user experience, and user-centered design. Make it simple. Make it easy. Don't make me think!

Calvin Mooers reminds us that design of a useful information system requires a deep understanding of users and their social context. We cannot assume people will *want* our information, even if we know they *need* our information. Behind most failed web sites, intranets, and interactive products lie misguided models of users and their information-seeking behavior. Users are complex. Users are social. And so is information.

Defining Information

What is information? Consult a dictionary and enter a strange loop of circular definitions resembling the impossible structures of M.C. Escher, shown in Figure 3-1. Data is information is knowledge is information is data. Ask an expert and receive a philosophical treatise on the fine distinctions between data, information, knowledge, and wisdom. Ask a colleague and they'll question your sanity. But go ahead anyway. Ask someone to define information. Then poke holes in their definitions. Keep at it. Don't let them off the hook. I'll bet it's easy and fun, in a disturbing sort of way, like shooting fish in a barrel.

Our inability to precisely answer this question speaks volumes about the subject. Information surrounds us. We can cite examples ad infinitum: articles, books, cartoons, databases, encyclopedias, files, gestures, holograms, images, journals, knowledge bases, laws, maps, numbers, ontologies, paintings, quizzes, rules, signs, texts, users, variables, web sites, xeroxes, yaks, and zebras. We use information. We create information. But we can't draw a circle around the category and agree what's in and out. Take yaks and zebras for instance. Scholars argue that under the right circumstances, animals can enter the category we call documents. We'll revisit this bizarre claim later, but for now, let's agree to disagree about the definition of information.

---

* "How Hardwired Is Human Behavior?" by Nigel Nicholson. *Harvard Business Review*, July/ August 1998.

Figure 3-1. Relativity (left) and Sky and Water I (right) by M.C. Escher (© 2005 The M. C. Escher Company-Holland. All rights reserved. www.mcescher.com)

It's not that good people haven't tried to crack this nut. In fact, the field of information science was first defined in the early 1960s as:

> The science that investigates the properties and behavior of information, the forces governing the flow of information, and the means of processing information for optimum accessibility and usability. The processes include the origination, dissemination, collection, organization, storage, retrieval, interpretation, and use of information.[*]

Since then, working definitions have emerged within the field:

- Data. A string of identified but unevaluated symbols.
- Information. Evaluated, validated, or useful data.
- Knowledge. Information in the context of understanding.

But they only lead to more questions. Can evaluation turn data into information? Or is information defined by its value to the end user? Is it data that makes a difference? How about the knowledge we seek to manage? Can knowledge (and understanding) even exist outside the mind? We conflate distinctions of source, process, impact, and location. Yet we muddle through. We negotiate. We translate. We communicate. And therein lies the key to this Tower of Babel. Information is about communication. It involves the exchange of symbols, ideas, messages, and meaning between people. As such, it's characterized by ambiguity, redundancy, inefficiency, error, and indescribable beauty.

---

[*] "Information Science: What is it?" by Harold Borko. *American Documentation*, 1968.

Communication is among humanity's greatest gifts. Without it, we would always be alone, trapped in our own thoughts and constrained by our own limitations. With it, we enjoy an amazing extension of the human nervous system. A child runs toward a street chasing a ball. The driver of an approaching car is blinded by the sun. A neighbor yells a single word. Stop! Communication is first and foremost about cooperation. It is evolutionary evidence that, in the words of Ben Franklin, "we must all hang together, or assuredly we shall all hang separately."[*] For countless millennia, small groups of humans have used gestural and verbal communication for collaborative hunting, gathering, fighting, parenting, learning, and decision-making.

Communication is the backbone of all human society from ancient tribes to modern nations. And, information is the principal ingredient that enables cooperation to scale from clans with a few dozen members to an interconnected global economy of billions. Information allows us to communicate across time and space. From marks on bark to etchings in silicon, we're able to share observations, experience, insight, and emotion. Documents are talking objects. They make possible the wonders of art, business, engineering, government, law, literature, and science. Documents enable us to stand on the shoulders of giants. Information is heady stuff indeed.

Yet when we try to define information, we become lost in a hall of mirrors occupied by human reflections, and we're back to the illusions and infinite loops of M.C. Escher. To escape this prison of relativity, we must abandon our discussions of disembodied, decontextualized, generic information. We must add substance and specificity. In short, we must classify. For once we categorize and contextualize, definitions come easy. Consider, for instance, a recipe book. It contains a collection of recipes that specify instructions and ingredients. It is typically a printed, bound document used by a cook in a kitchen for selecting and preparing meals. It provides multiple ways to find recipes, often by cooking method and type of cuisine. It includes a table of contents and an index.

This example illustrates the power and pervasiveness of genre. The term *recipe book* conjures up a specific image complete with format, structure, content, organization, context, and purpose. When we talk about novels, speeches, movies, magazines, letters, emails, billboards, blogs, and web sites, we rely on genre as shorthand to indicate both the message and the medium. Of course, new technologies complicate matters. Once upon a

---

[*] According to the Wikipedia, there is no evidence that Ben Franklin ever made this statement: *http://en.wikipedia.org/wiki/United_States_Declaration_of_Independence*.

time, a story was an oral and aural experience, spoken directly from story-teller to listener, stored in human memory, and passed down through generations. This type of "story" enjoyed monopoly power for between 40,000 and 2,000,000 years. We're not exactly sure since we have no records of this "pre-history." In any case, around 5,000 years ago we invented written language and complicated things. We now had to qualify whether we "heard a story" or "read a story." Then, in the last 30 years, personal computers and the Internet happened. Suddenly, stories could flow from spoken word to printed text to digital document, and back again. A story could be encoded into a series of bits, transported around the world at the speed of light, and stored on a multitude of media. *War and Peace* on a laptop. *The Odyssey* on a flash drive. *The Bible* on a Treo.

Make our recipe book available online and it's no longer *just* a book. It becomes an interactive product and database with a user interface for search and navigation. It's available on desktop computers and mobile devices around the world. And thanks to Google's keyword search, each recipe has become a discrete findable object. Users may access individual recipes without experiencing the broader collection we call a book. In fact, our recipe book has mutated into something else, and we're not sure what to call it. Perhaps it's an online cookbook, a recipe collection, or a recipe archive. Or maybe it's just a web site with a branded name like *epicurious.com*. A Google search elicits even stranger real world examples including Recipe Goldmine, Recipe Cottage, and RecipeLand. Clearly, the Web has confused our notions of genre. The recipes survive but the book is blown to bits. Technology and genre are intertwined. Books. Television. The Web. The way we experience the message is shaped by the medium. And the ways we define information are shaped by the properties of that medium and the context of use.

Our confusion today is but one sign of the turbulence in our media landscape being wrought by the relentless drive of Moore's Law towards faster, smaller, cheaper computer processors. Today Google and the World Wide Web dominate our information universe. Tomorrow will be different. But before we look ahead, it's worth looking back at the universe of Calvin Mooers and the science of information retrieval.

Information Retrieval

When Calvin Mooers coined the term "information retrieval" in 1948, Hollerith (IBM) punch cards were the state of the art. First invented in 1896 by Henry P. Stamford, these edge-notched punch cards enabled people to search insurance records and library collections by metadata. Each notch constituted a descriptor (also known as an index term or metadata tag). In early versions, the user would thread a 16 inch needle through a stack of cards. The relevant notched cards would drop from the collection. A subsequent search of this result set enabled further narrowing (the Boolean AND). Non-relevant cards retrieved by this process were called "false drops," a term we still use today.

To those of us living in the age of Google, the world of punch cards seems distant and quaint. In fact, things have happened so fast in recent years, even 1993 seems like a lifetime ago. Back then, I was learning "online searching" at the University of Michigan's School of Information and Library Studies. We searched through databases via dumb terminals connected to the Dialog company's mainframe. Results were output to a dot matrix printer. And Dialog charged by the minute. This made searching quite stressful. Mistakes were costly in time and money. So, we'd spend an hour or more in the library beforehand, consulting printed thesauri for descriptors, considering how to combine Boolean operators most efficiently, and plotting our overall search strategy. A computer's time was more precious than a human's, so we sweated every keyword.

Meanwhile, NCSA was developing the first graphical, multimedia interface to the World Wide Web, released as the Mosaic web browser in 1993. This killer application launched the Internet revolution that transformed our relationship with information systems. A browser for every desktop. A web site for every company. Billions of pages searchable via Google. For free. And hundreds of millions of untrained users searching for digital cameras, scientific papers, uncensored news, and photos of Britney Spears. The technology and context for retrieval changed radically. And yet, the central challenges and principles of information retrieval, forged in the decades between punch cards and web browsers, remain valid and important. And because they derive from the fundamental nature of language and meaning, they are unlikely to change anytime soon.

At the heart of these challenges and principles lies the concept of relevance. Simply put, relevant results are those which are interesting and useful to users. Precision and recall, our most basic measures of effectiveness, are built upon this common-sense definition, as shown in Figure 3-2. Precision measures how well a system retrieves *only* the relevant documents. Recall measures how well a system retrieves *all* the relevant documents.

The relative importance of these metrics varies based on the type of search. For the *sample search* in which a few good documents are sufficient, precision outweighs recall. Most Google searchers, for example, want a few good results fast without sifting through false drops. Precision is even more important for the known-item or *existence search* in which a specific document (or web site) is desired. In fact, this type of search has more in

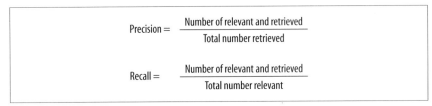

$$\text{Precision} = \frac{\text{Number of relevant and retrieved}}{\text{Total number retrieved}}$$

$$\text{Recall} = \frac{\text{Number of relevant and retrieved}}{\text{Total number relevant}}$$

Figure 3-2. Definitions of precision and recall

common with data retrieval than information retrieval—because there is a single, correct answer. But for the *exhaustive search* when all or nearly all relevant documents are desired, recall is the key metric. Lawyers and researchers are willing to sacrifice precision in the interest of finding the smoking gun or the data that makes a difference. Of course, recall is tricky to measure because it requires a count of the total number of relevant documents in a collection: not so hard with a few hundred punch cards but pretty tough with several billion web pages.

This brings us to the subject of scale. In information retrieval, size matters, and we only learned recently how much. Through the 1960s and 70s, when the first full-text search systems were developed, experiments using IBM's Storage and Information Retrieval System (STAIRS) showed both precision and recall to run as high as 75 to 80%. This made IBM very happy and fueled predictions about the end of metadata. Why spend time and money having humans apply index terms when automatic full-text retrieval worked as well or better? Fire your librarians. Buy IBM. The future is automated.

Unfortunately, there was a fatal flaw in the experiments. They were conducted on small collections of a few hundred documents, and the assumption that these results applied to large collections was mistaken. In the 1980s, researchers David C. Blair and M.E. Maron evaluated a large, operational full-text litigation support system containing roughly 40,000 documents with 350,000 pages of text.[*] The lawyers using this system regarded 75% recall as essential to defense of the case, and believed the system met that standard. But Blair and Maron showed that while precision remained high (around 80%), recall averaged a miserable 20%. The system was retrieving only 1 of 5 relevant documents. And this was with trained searchers! This exceptionally large and rigorous study exposed a fundamental challenge: recall falls dramatically as the collection increases in size.[†] And since

---

[*] "An Evaluation of Retrieval Effectiveness for a Full-Text Document Retrieval System" by David C. Blair and M.E. Maron. *Communications of the ACM*, March 1985.

[†] Due to the need for researchers to manually evaluate the relevance of large numbers of documents, this study cost (adjusted for inflation) over a million dollars. Needless to say, few retrieval experiments of this scale have been conducted since.

the holdings of many web sites, intranets, and digital collections far exceeds 40,000 documents, these findings are clearly relevant today. Size matters. Big time. But why? And what happens in larger collections of 400,000 or 4,000,000 documents? Does precision remain high? Does recall drop further? For those answers, we must turn to the complex adaptive network we call language.

Language and Representation

Words intended to represent concepts: that is the questionable foundation upon which information retrieval is built. Words in the content. Words in the query. Even collections of images and software and physical objects rely on words in the form of metadata for representation and retrieval. And words are imprecise, ambiguous, indeterminate, vague, opaque; you get the picture. Our language bubbles with synonyms, homonyms, acronyms, and even contronyms (words with contradictory meanings in different contexts such as sanction, cleave, and bi-weekly). And this is before we even talk about the epic numbers of spelling errors committed on a daily basis. In *The Mother Tongue*, author Bill Bryson shares a wealth of colorful facts about language, including:

> The residents of the Trobriand Islands of Papua New Guinea have a hundred words for yams, while the Maoris of New Zealand have thirty-five words for dung.

> In the OED, round alone (that is without variants like rounded and roundup) takes 7 pages to define or about 15,000 words of text.

> English retains probably the richest vocabulary, and most diverse shading of meanings, of any language....No other language has so many words all saying the same thing.

Interestingly, when this ambiguity of language is subjected to statistical analysis, familiar patterns indicative of power laws, shown in Figure 3-3, emerge. First observed by the Italian economist Vilfredo Pareto in the early 1900s, power laws result in many small events coexisting with a few large events. Later summed up as Pareto's Principle or the 80/20 Rule, power laws have since been applied to a wide variety of phenomenon including wealth disparity (80% of money is earned by 20% of the population), scientific publishing (a small number of journals contribute the vast percentage of scientific output), and web site popularity (80% of links on the Web point to only 15% of web pages).[*]

---

[*] *Linked: The New Science of Networks* by Albert-Laszlo Barabasi. Perseus (2002), p. 66.

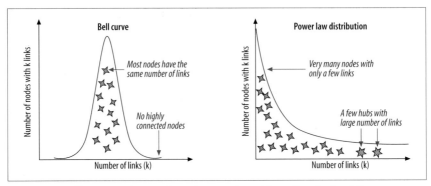

Figure 3-3. Bell curves and power laws (image adapted from Barabasi, p.71)

Bell curves and not power laws are the norm in nature. If human height followed a power law distribution, most of us would be really short, but at least one of us would be over 8,000 feet tall.* Power laws only show up in complex networks that exhibit self-organization and emergent behavior. Language happens to be one of these networks, and the implications for retrieval are significant.

The most famous study of power laws in the English language was conducted by Harvard linguistics professor George Kingsley Zipf in the early 1900s. By analyzing large texts, Zipf found that a few words occur very often and many words occur very rarely. The two most frequent words can account for 10% of occurrences, the top six for 20%, and the top 50 for 50%. Zipf postulated this occurred as a result of competition between forces for unification (general words with many meanings) and diversification (specific words with precise meaning). In the context of retrieval, we might interpret these as the forces of description and discrimination.† The force of description dictates that the intellectual content of documents should be described as completely as possible. The force of discrimination dictates that documents should be distinguished from other documents in the system. Full text is biased towards description. Unique identifiers such as ISBNs (and Zip Codes) offer perfect discrimination but no descriptive value. Metadata fields (e.g., title, author, publisher) and controlled vocabularies (e.g., subject, category, format, audience) hold the middle ground.

The upshot of all this analysis is that while recall fails fastest, precision also drops precipitously as full-text retrieval systems grow larger. In the "com-

---

* Barabasi, p. 67.

† "The Challenge of Commercial Document Retrieval, Part I" by David C. Blair (2002). *Information Processing & Management*, vol. 38, p.273–291.

puting" example that follows, the larger system returns too many results with too many meanings. Without asking the user to add keywords, use Boolean operators, or specify context, there's no way for the system to know which meaning the user intends. This problem is further amplified by the fact that when we enter "computing" as a keyword, we're generally looking for documents *about* computing and not just documents that contain the word computing. Though relevance ranking algorithms can factor in the location and frequency of word occurrence, there is no way for software to accurately determine *aboutness*.

1000 docs in system   100 documents contain the word "computing"
"computing" used 10 different ways.

100,000 docs in system   7,100 documents contain the word "computing"
"computing" used in 84 different ways.
—*The Challenge of Commercial Document Retrieval*
by David Blair (2002), p.279.

That's where metadata enters the picture. Metadata tags applied by humans can indicate aboutness thereby improving precision. This is one of Google's secrets for success. Google's PageRank algorithm recognizes inbound links constructed by humans to be an excellent indicator of aboutness. Google loves metadata. Controlled vocabularies (organized lists of approved words and phrases) for populating metadata fields can further improve precision through their discriminatory power. And the specification of equivalence, hierarchical, and associative relationships can enhance recall by linking synonyms, acronyms, misspellings, and broader, narrower, and related terms, as shown in Figure 3-4.

Controlled vocabularies help retrieval systems to manage the challenges of ambiguity and meaning inherent in language. And they become increasingly valuable as systems grow larger. Unfortunately, centralized manual tagging efforts also become prohibitively expensive and time-consuming for most large-scale applications. So they often can't be used where they're needed the most. For all these reasons, information retrieval is an uphill battle. Sometimes we do make progress. Google's multi-algorithmic approach that combines full text, metadata, and popularity measures is the most striking example in recent years. But don't hold your breath for similar break throughs. Despite the hype surrounding artificial intelligence, Bayesian pat-

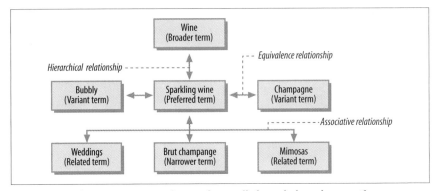

Figure 3-4. A thesaurus is a special type of controlled vocabulary that specifies equivalence, hierarchical, and associative relationships

tern matching, and information visualization, computers aren't even close to extracting or understanding or visually representing meaning. For as long as humans use language to communicate, information retrieval will be remain a messy, imperfect business.

But before you despair about the sorry state of information retrieval and its implications for search on your web site or intranet, take a deep breath and sit down. Because it gets worse. Much, much worse. Remember Calvin Mooers and his pesky law about the pain of having information? Well, he was onto something far more formidable and irksome than the ambiguity in language. Calvin Mooers was onto the people problem.

The People Problem

Early studies of information retrieval systems featured quantitative approaches characteristic of the physical sciences. Mathematical formulas for precision and recall created an aura of objectivity for the nascent field of information science. And yet behind every formula lurked a variable that resisted isolation. Today we call this infuriating variable "the user" and we recognize that research must integrate rather than isolate the goals, behaviors, and idiosyncrasies of the people who use the systems.

Upon admitting the people problem, relevance was the first casualty, for measures of relevance are highly subjective. Ask individuals to evaluate the relevance of search results, and their responses will vary according to what they already know and what they want to know. Even the same individual may evaluate the same results differently as her knowledge and interest changes over time. Now this doesn't mean we should dismiss the metrics of precision and recall. For defined audiences and contexts (e.g., engineers using the HP intranet), sufficient agreement among users exists to make relevance measures meaningful. But we should proceed with an understanding that relevance is subjective, situational, and dynamic. Like beauty, relevance exists in the eye of the beholder.

Perhaps the most important thing we know about users is that they vigorously embrace what our friend George Kingsley Zipf called the Principle of Least Effort:

> Each individual will adopt a course of action that will involve the expenditure of the probably least average of his work (by definition, least effort).

This fits with Calvin Mooers' insight that people will not seek information that makes their jobs harder (even if it may benefit the organization they work for). And it explains the relentless migration to more accessible, usable information systems. Why visit the library when Google's on your desktop? In fact, numerous studies have shown users are often willing to sacrifice information quality for accessibility.* This fast food approach to information consumption drives librarians crazy. "Our information is healthier and tastes better too" they shout. But nobody listens. We're too busy Googling.

However, before we grow too smug about our instinctual "optimization algorithms," perhaps we should question the sanity of this fast food diet. After all, there's a fine line between the wisdom of crowds and the ignorance of mobs. Maybe our willingness to trade quality for accessibility is not entirely rational. In fact, there's a whole lot of evidence that human behavior is often not rational or optimal. At best, we "satisfice" under conditions of "bounded rationality." Nobel Laureate Herbert Simon coined these terms in the 1950s to explain the divergence between economic models built on theories of rational decision-making and the unruliness of reality. People are not perfect nor perfectly predictable. Any model that assumes otherwise is doomed to failure.

More recently, research in human-computer interaction has further exposed the soft underbelly of the people problem. A Stanford study entitled "Silicon Sycophants" showed that people respond positively to flattery from computers.† In a series of tests, users rated system performance more highly when the system said nice things about the user. This held true even when users were told to expect gratuitous flattery. In another Stanford experi-

---

* "Seeking Information In Order to Produce Information: An Empirical Study at Hewlett Packard Labs" by Sandra Hirsh and Jamie Dinkleacker. *Journal of the American Society for Information Science and Technology*, July 2004.

† "Silicon Sycophants: the Effects of Computers that Flatter" by B.J. Fogg and Clifford Nass (1997). *International Journal of Human-Computer Studies*, vol. 46.

ment, Clifford Nass showed that people are polite to computers.[*] After completing several tasks using a computer system, subjects were instructed to evaluate system performance. Responses solicited on that same computer were significantly more positive than those solicited on a different computer or via paper and pencil. Apparently, people were reluctant to criticize the computer to its face. And finally, even Don Norman has gone soft on us with his latest book about *Emotional Design* which presents scientific evidence that attractive things work better. Since being happy broadens our thought processes and facilitates creative thinking, attractive products that make us happy can improve our ability to use them. In effect, they work better because we work better. Small gifts (and flattery) can have similar positive effects. But why are we so susceptible to these superficial elements? How can such smart beings be so shallow?

The answers reside in the fields of neuroscience and evolutionary psychology, both of which strive to discover and understand the design of the human mind. In *Mind Wide Open*, Steven Johnson takes us on a tour of today's cutting-edge brain research. He explains that the brain is "an ecosystem with modules simultaneously competing and relying on one another" and notes that "a fundamental tension in the human brain lies in the battle between the amygdala and the neocortex—the emotional center wrestling for control with the seat of reason." In other words, rationality must compete with what we affectionately call our "lizard brain" and rationality doesn't always win. In fact, as Don Norman notes:

> Much of human behavior is subconscious, beneath conscious awareness. Consciousness comes late, both in evolution and also in the way the brain processes information; many judgments have already been determined before they reach consciousness.[†]

This is where neuroscience meets evolutionary psychology, a relatively new field concisely described by Nigel Nicholson of the London Business School:

> New fields don't emerge in a flash, and evolutionary psychology—sometimes called *modern Darwinism*—is no exception. But over the past several years, evolutionary psychology as a discipline has gathered both momentum and respect. A convergence of research and discoveries in genetics, neuropsychology, and paleobiology, among other sciences, evolutionary psychology holds that although human beings today inhabit a thoroughly modern world of space exploration and virtual realities, they do so with the ingrained mentality of Stone Age hunter-gatherers.[‡]

---

[*] "Etiquette Equality: Exhibitions and Expectations of Computer Politeness" by Clifford Nass. *Communications of the ACM*, April 2004.

[†] *Emotional Design* by Don Norman. Perseus (2004), p. 11.

[‡] "How Hardwired is Human Behavior?" by Nigel Nicholson (1998). *Harvard Business Review*, p. 135.

In other words, you can take the person out of the Stone Age, but you can't take the Stone Age out of the person. Our neural circuits and natural instincts were designed to solve problems faced by our ancestors over millions of years of evolution. More than 99% of our species' evolutionary history (about 10 million years) was spent living in hunter-gatherer societies. The world we know—filled with roads, grocery stores, factories, schools, cell phones, web sites, and nation states—has lasted for only the blink of an eye. Agriculture emerged only 10,000 years ago. The industrial revolution is a mere 200 years old. The information age has just begun. We have transformed our environment but not ourselves. Technology moves fast. Evolution moves slow.

In exploring the managerial implications of evolutionary psychology, Nicholson also sheds light on the information sharing behavior we call gossip:

> The individuals who ruled the clan and controlled the resources were always changing. Survivors were those who were savvy enough to anticipate power shifts and swiftly adjust to them...They were savvy because they engaged in, and likely showed a skill for, gossip. Even in today's office environment, we can observe that expert gossips time and again know key information before everyone else.[*]

Despite huge investments in information and communication technology, we still rely heavily on informal person-to-person networks known as "the grapevine." And we often trust this "unofficial news" more than the "official story." Of course, we've co-opted the technology infrastructure, extending the locus of gossip from the water cooler to cyberspace—email, instant messaging, cell phones, text messaging, listservs, weblogs—at the heart of many of today's killer applications lies the power and prevalence of gossip. It may not be ideal with respect to ethics or efficiency, but it's the way people are wired, and the blueprint is ancient and immutable. Politicians capitalize on this quality of human nature with grassroots, word-of-mouth campaigns. Advertisers embrace viral marketing methods that spread contagious memes through social networks. And information innovators from Amazon and Google to Flickr (Figure 3-5) and del.icio.us tap into the gift of gossip and the power of popularity to inspire participation and improve information retrieval.

But perhaps retrieval isn't the best word to describe the myriad ways we interact with information today. After all, thanks to Moore's Law, our environment has changed dramatically since the days of punch cards and mainframes. And in keeping with Mooers' Law, we are now more willing to

---

[*] Nicholson (1998), p. 141.

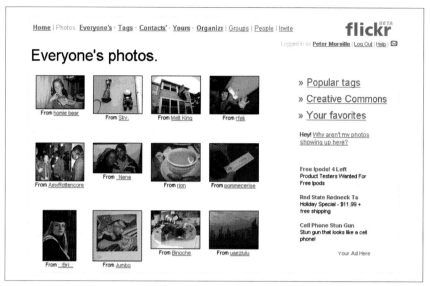

Figure 3-5. Flickr is a collaborative, highly contagious, metadata-driven, web-based image sharing and retrieval application

embrace the social and psychological dimensions of information seeking behavior. We need a phrase and a field that remembers the past, fits the present, and anticipates the future. In short, we need information interaction.

Information Interaction

In 1995, Nahum Gershon coined the term "Human Information Interaction" (HII) to denote "how human beings interact with, relate to, and process information regardless of the medium connecting the two." Since then, the term has been widely adopted by the traditional information science and retrieval communities. Gary Marchionini of the UNC School of Information and Library Science explains "the IR problem itself has fundamentally changed and a new paradigm of information interaction has emerged."*

This paradigm is characterized by highly interactive interfaces, user-centered methods, and a sensitivity to the dynamic, multi-channel nature of information seeking behavior. Researchers in Human Information Interaction draw insight and inspiration from the field of Human Computer Inter-

---

* "From Information Retrieval to Information Interaction" by Gary Marchionini. Available from *http://www.ils.unc.edu/~march/ECIR.pdf.*

action (HCI) while recognizing they face unique challenges. As Elaine Toms suggests, "(the) unstructured, complex problem-solving task (of information seeking) cannot be reduced in a predictable way to a set of routine Goals, Operators, Methods, and Selections (GOMS)."* In other words, the complexity of information interaction is not expressed well in typical models of human-computer interaction. HCI approaches are optimal for software applications and interfaces where designers can exercise great control over form and function. HII approaches are optimal for networked information systems where control is sacrificed for interoperability. In such environments, users may find and interact with information objects through a variety of devices and interfaces. The emphasis shifts from interface to information.

Fortunately, we're not starting from scratch. Thanks to pioneers who anticipated the current paradigm, we've inherited a wealth of information interaction information. In particular, Marcia J. Bates deserves credit for shaping our understanding of information seeking behavior. In a 1989 article entitled "The Design of Browsing and Berrypicking Techniques for the Online Search Interface," Marcia Bates exposed the inadequacy of the classic information retrieval model characterized by a single query, shown in Figure 3-6.

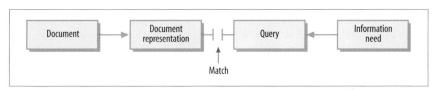

Figure 3-6. The classic information retrieval model

Instead, she proposed a berrypicking model that recognizes the iterative and interactive nature of the information seeking process. Bates understood that the query and the information need itself evolve as users interact with documents and search systems. She also recognized that since relevant documents (like berries) tend to be scattered, users move fluidly between search and browse modes, relying on a rich variety of strategies including footnote chasing, area scanning, and citation, subject, and author searching, as shown in Figure 3-7.

In short, Bates described information seeking behavior on today's Web, back in 1989. Google relies on the citations we call "inbound links." Blogs support "backward chaining" through TrackBack. Flickr and del.icio.us

* "Information Interaction: Providing a Framework for Information Architecture" by Elaine G. Toms. *Journal of the American Society for Information Science and Technology*, August 2002, p. 857.

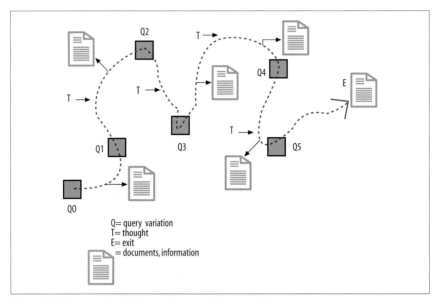

Figure 3-7. Marcia Bates' berrypicking, evolving search

allow us to pivot on subject or author. The Web allows our information seeking to grow more iterative and interactive with each innovation. The berrypicking model is more relevant today than ever.

By studying behavior with an open mind, Marcia Bates learned to see information systems and their human users from a new perspective. In fact, her insights laid the foundation for modern studies at the intersection of evolutionary psychology and information seeking. The thread she began with "berrypicking" was picked up by Xerox PARC researchers Peter Pirolli and Stuart Card in their study of information foraging. They explain "we use the term 'foraging' both to conjure up the metaphor of organisms browsing for sustenance and to indicate a connection to the more technical optimal foraging theory found in biology and anthropology."[*] Their studies in information foraging have been noted by Jakob Nielsen as vitally important in the age of Google.[†] And their concept of "information scent" has entered the vernacular of web design.

---

[*] "Information Foraging in Information Access Environments" by Peter Pirolli and Stuart Card. *Proceedings of the Conference on Human Factors in Computing Systems*, CHI 1995, p. 51–58.

[†] "Information Foraging: Why Google Makes People Leave Your Site Faster" by Jakob Nielsen. From *http://www.useit.com/alertbox/20030630.html.*

Today, researchers are probing the adaptive behavior of collaborative foraging in nature for insights into collaborative filtering on the Web. As one investigator explains:

> The behavior of honey bees in a hive generates an emergent structure, using optimal foraging strategies that are enriched by collaboration. Honey bees use a set of "dance" movements to communicate the direction, distance, and richness of pollen and nectar patches. This information is incorporated into the hive knowledge....Likewise, collaborative foraging agents on the Web can form emergent network structures in order to describe and organize pages.[*]

And, scientists at the University of Washington are using a multidimensional approach called Cognitive Work Analysis to study collaborative information interaction:

> Most researchers in human-information behavior have elected to conduct their work within either the psychological or the social approach. However, a growing number of researchers believe that for a thorough understanding of human-information interaction, both are necessary, and possibly other approaches as well....One of the motivations behind this approach is the need to account for the complexity that exists in human-information interaction in the real world.[†]

And, of course, Marcia Bates continues to break new ground with her research investigations aimed at developing an integrated model of information seeking and searching that incorporates aesthetic, biological, historical, psychological, social, and even spiritual layers of understanding. She continues to ask tough questions:

> Why do physicians not use the medical literature, rather than relying on the drug company salesman for information about a new drug? Why will our students not get up and walk a hundred meters to access a key journal article in the library? The natural human tendency in information seeking is to fall back on passive and sampling and selecting behaviors derived from millions of years of [evolution]....It is not surprising, then, that the methods of access designed by librarians are generally little used.[‡]

In the spirit of Calvin Mooers, Bates makes painfully honest diagnoses, and follows up with creative prescriptions for the future. She explains why we

---

[*] "A Collaborative Foraging Approach to Web Browsing Enrichment" by Stephen Schultze. CHI April 20–25, 2002.

[†] "A Multidimensional Approach to the Study of Human Information Interaction: A Case Study of Collaborative Information Retrieval" by Raya Fidel, Annelise Mark Pejtersen, Bryan Cleal, and Harry Bruce. *Journal of the American Society for Information Science and Technology*, September 2004.

[‡] "Towards an Integrated Model of Information Seeking and Searching" by Marcia J. Bates. Keynote for The Fourth International Conference on Information Needs, Seeking and Use in Different Contexts, Lisbon, Portugal, September 11–13, 2002.

value gossip so highly, and then encourages us to design gossip into our systems. It's not just about retrieval. We must embrace both push and pull. We must utilize the full spectrum of interaction.

Finally, HII shifts emphasis from technology, interface, and medium to the information objects themselves. In recent years, Andrew Dillon and Misha Vaughan have begun exploring the concept of information shape and the emergent property of genre.[*] And Elaine Toms has identified the importance of *cues*, which:

> ...serve as landmarks that influence the direction a user takes in scanning information. Selected words or phrases embedded in the text cause a searcher to examine a segment of text. This...suggests the existence of *affordances* in the text....Much like the distinctive profiles of downtown Manhattan and Toronto that provide valuable cues about the identity of those cityscapes, the physical landscape of a document also contains distinctive, salient features that inform users about a document's identity.[†]

In the literature of information shape and genre, we suddenly find ourselves back at the intersection of physical and digital, talking about document landscapes, textual landmarks, and wayfinding in cyberspace. Of course, this convergence is accelerating in accord with Moore's Law. The boundaries between information and objects blur more each day. To observe this in action, keep an eye on Google, whose stated mission is "to organize the world's information and make it universally accessible and useful."

You see, the tricky thing about Google is they keep changing their definition of information. First, it was just web sites. Then images, online discussions, blogs, news, and products entered the fold. Then phone numbers, addresses, street maps, and FedEx tracking data. Then, the contents of your desktop computer. Then, the contents of the world's largest research libraries. Millions of books transformed into bytes. And acquisitions such as Keyhole, a company specializing in satellite imagery software, and Dodgeball, a pioneer in mobile social software, suggest Google has big plans for information, plans that reach far beyond what we normally think of as the Web.

Now, Calvin Mooers might ask whether this promised land of pervasive computing and ambient information is as desirable as we're led to believe. Will our information environments of tomorrow really be less painful and troublesome than those of today? Is more really more or less? How will

---

[*] "It's the Journey and the Destination: Shape and the Emergent Property of Genre in Evaluating Digital Documents" by Andrew Dillon and Misha Vaughan (1997). *New Review of Multimedia and Hypermedia*, vol. 3.

[†] "Recognizing Digital Genre" by Elaine G. Toms. *Bulletin of the American Society for Information Science and Technology*, December/January 2001.

humans respond to such a wealth of information? These are important questions we will answer the hard way by surfing ahead at breakneck speed on the waves of the technology tsunami that's powered by Moore's Law.

CHAPTER 4

Intertwingled

*Intertwingularity is not generally
acknowledged—people keep pretending they
can make things deeply hierarchical,
categorizable and sequential when they
can't. Everything is deeply intertwingled.*
—Theodor Holm Nelson

As a sociology student at Harvard in the early 1960s, Ted Nelson enrolled in a computer course for the humanities that changed his life. For his term project, he tried to develop a text-handling system that would enable writers to edit and compare their work easily. Considering he was coding on a mainframe in Assembler language before word processing had been invented, it's no surprise his attempt fell short. Despite this early setback, Ted was captivated by the potential of nonsequential text to transform how we organize and share ideas. His pioneering work on "hypertext" and "hypermedia" laid an intellectual foundation for the World Wide Web, and his views on "intertwingularity" will haunt the house of ubicomp for many years to come.

We experience Nelson's intertwingularity every time we click a hypertext link. We move fluidly between different pages, documents, sites, authors, formats, and topics. In this nonlinear world, the contrasts can be dramatic. A single blog post may link to an article about dinosaurs, a pornographic video, a presidential speech, and a funny song about cabbage. We routinely travel vast semantic distances in the space of a second, and these dramatic transitions aren't limited to the Web. Our remote controls put hundreds of television channels at our fingertips. Terrorism on CNN. Click. Sumo wrestling on ESPN. Click. *Sesame Street* on PBS. Click. And our cell phones relentlessly punctuate the flow of daily life. One minute we're playing soccer with our kids at the neighborhood park. Seconds later we're in the midst of a business crisis half way around the world. The juxtapositions are worthy of shock and awe. Business and pleasure. Reality and fiction. Humor and horror. And yet, we're not shocked. We've become accustomed to dramatic transition. We expect it. We enjoy it. We're addicted.

Hypermedia technologies permeate our environment, shaping a bizarre hyper-reality that delivers information and commands attention. And even as we complain of information anxiety, we're about to elevate intertwingularity to a whole new level with the advent of "ubiquitous computing." The late Mark Weiser, formerly chief technology officer at Xerox PARC, coined the term in 1988 to define a future in which PCs are replaced with tiny, invisible computers embedded in everyday objects. So, whether we call it ubiquitous, pervasive, mobile, embedded, invisible, ambient, or calm computing, the vision is nothing new. What's new is the rapid transformation of this vision into reality. It's really happening, right now. Where Moore's Law meets Metcalfe's Law, we've reached a tipping point, and there's no going back. Faster, smaller, cheaper processors and devices. A rich tapestry of communication networks with ever-increasing bandwidth. A constant stream of acronyms tumbling into our vernacular: GPS, RFID, MEMS, IPv6, UWB. We don't need a crystal ball to see the road ahead. As William Gibson warned us "The future exists today. It's just unevenly distributed."

Metcalfe's Law

Metcalfe's Law states that the usefulness, or utility, of a network equals the square of the number of users. In other words, the value of networked systems (e.g., telephone, fax, email, Web) grows exponentially as the user population increases in a linear manner.

My fascination with this *future present* dwells at the crossroads of ubiquitous computing and the Internet. We're creating new interfaces to export networked information while simultaneously importing vast amounts of data about the real world into our networks. Familiar boundaries blur in this great intertwingling. Toilets sprout sensors. Objects consume their own metadata. Ambient devices, findable objects, tangible bits, wearables, implants, and ingestibles are just some of the strange mutations residing in this borderlands of atoms and bits. They are signposts on the road to ambient findability, a realm in which we can find anyone or anything from anywhere at anytime. Of course, ambient findability is not necessarily a goal.

We may have serious reservations about life in the global Panopticon.* And from a practical perspective, it's an unreachable destination. Perfect findability is unattainable. And yet, we're surely headed in the general direction of the unexplored territory of ambient findability. So strap on your seatbelts, power up your smartphones, and prepare for turbulence. Beyond this place, there be dragons. Or is it streets paved with silicon? Either way, we'll soon find out.

Everyware

In April 2001, after the agonizing process of closing my former company, I managed to escape into the sanctuary of Yosemite National Park. I enjoyed the romantic notion of figuring out what to do with the rest of my life while hiking in the wilderness. So, armed with a bottle of water and some beef jerky, I headed for the snowy peaks in search of transcendental moments and healing visions. Upon reaching the summit, I found myself alone, amidst the most breathtaking panorama I have ever seen. I sat for a while, enjoying the beauty and tranquility of the Sierra Nevada mountains. Then, I reached into my pocket, pulled out my cell phone, and called my mom. Can you hear me now?

These days, people use cell phones everywhere: in planes, trains, automobiles, grocery stores, golf courses, and bathtubs. During a half-marathon last summer, I saw a fellow runner with a cell phone held to his sweaty ear. In today's society, such behavior barely raises eyebrows. Conspicuous consumption is hip. Leather holsters, swivel belt clips, colored faceplates, and personalized ringtones transform consumer appliance into hi-tech fashion statement: everyware for everybody who's anybody. Until yesterday. Haven't you heard? Cell phones are passé. GSM smart phones are where it's at. Web, email, calendar, contacts, stereo, camera, television, and global positioning system in a single device. Moblogging from a ski lift in the Swiss Alps? Now that's cool. Checking email while driving? Not so cool, though I'm guilty as charged. As William Gibson says, "the street finds its own use for things." And that's part of the fun. The search space for novel uses of mobile devices is immense and stretches well beyond findability into art, business, education, entertainment, healthcare, politics, and warfare. We can read, write, buy, sell, talk, listen, work, play, attack, and defend.

---

* The Panopticon is a type of prison designed by the philosopher Jeremy Bentham. The concept of the design is to allow an observer to observe all prisoners without the prisoners being able to tell if they are being observed or not, thus conveying a "sentiment of an invisible omniscience." From *http://en.wikipedia.org/wiki/Panopticon*.

In *Smart Mobs*, Howard Rheingold emphasizes the potential of mobile communications to create a social revolution by enabling new forms of cooperation. He describes the emergent behavior exhibited by *thumb tribes* of connected teenagers: "the term 'swarming' was frequently used by the people I met in Helsinki to describe the cybernegotiated public flocking behavior of texting adolescents."[*] Rheingold notes that mobile devices enable groups of people to act in concert even if they don't know each other, and cites numerous examples of peaceful (and not so peaceful) public demonstrations from Manila to Seattle in which tens of thousands of protestors were mobilized and coordinated by cell phones and waves of text messages. In his book, Rheingold tends toward the sunny side of this future by asserting the wisdom of crowds:

> The right kinds of online social networks know more than the sum of their parts: connected and communicating in the right ways, populations of humans can exhibit a kind of collective intelligence.[†]

Of course, there's also a dark side to these technologies of cooperation. Smart phones don't always make for smart mobs. Groups of uninformed, agitated individuals can be dangerous and dumb, whether wielding pitch forks, flaming torches, or Nokia 7710s.

Fortunately, our mobile devices also enable us to become smarter (or at least more informed) individuals. We have instant access to an astonishing array of news sources, from CNN, Aljazeera, and the *Hindustan Times* to *slashdot.org* and *rageboy.com*. We can look up almost any fact from anywhere at anytime. Second and third and fourth opinions sprout like mushrooms after a rainfall. We have an unprecedented ability to choose our news and to see all sides of a story before making an informed decision. We can learn, and even better, we can remember, for our mobile devices also serve as outboard memory. They memorize schedules, names, addresses, phone numbers, passwords, birthdays, and grocery lists, so we don't have to. And increasingly, we rely on them. Our gadgets become part of our lives. The transition from nice to necessary can happen surprisingly fast, as novel use becomes expected facility. Consider the following:

- Student use of wireless laptops during classroom lectures for real-time reference (e.g., to fact check the professor's claims) and backchannel communications with fellow students (i.e., the digital equivalent of passing notes).

- Calling your spouse from the video store to gauge interest in a specific movie or from the grocery store to ask where to find the hot chocolate.

---

[*] *Smart Mobs* by Howard Rheingold. Perseus (2002), p. 13.
[†] Rheingold, p. 179.

- Googling a new acquaintance while waiting for him to arrive at a restaurant (he just called from the road to let you know he'd be five minutes late).
- Using a smartphone to check Amazon customer reviews (and prices) of books found while browsing inside a Barnes & Noble bookstore.
- Distributed, collaborative shopping by teenage girls using picture phones. How do you like this dress? Does this color look good on me? Should I buy one for you?

All of these uses and many more are becoming commonplace. Sometimes our mobile devices simply make us more efficient. Sometimes they cause fundamental and surprising changes in behavior. At the ragged edges of meatspace and cyberspace, the intertwingling has just begun. The users are inexperienced, the applications are immature, and the interfaces are exacting and temperamental. Tiny screens and keyboards don't make for optimal usability under the best of conditions. Even a teenager with nimble fingers and good eyes will interact better with a desktop computer than a smartphone. But mobile computing involves imperfect conditions: poor lighting, limited power, erratic motion, divided attention, and fractional connectivity. Try reading a white paper or typing an email message on a Treo while walking on the beach on a sunny day with your three-year-old daughter. Watch out for seagulls and hold on tight. Treos aren't waterproof, yet.

We will overcome some of these limitations. Batteries, which today contribute roughly 35% of a laptop computer's weight, will grow smaller, last longer, and recharge faster. Evolutionary progress in traditional lithium batteries continues while micro fuel cells and 3D architectures built with nanotech promise revolution. And in connectivity, the patchy mosaic of Bluetooth, Wi-Fi, and cellular data wireless (GSM/GPRS, CDMA) will inevitably be transformed into what we experience as a seamless utility. Already, Wi-Fi hot spots in offices and cafés are morphing into hot zones covering urban cores and in some cases entire metropolitan areas. And ultra-wideband (UWB) technologies promise effective wireless data rates of well over one gigabit per second, easily enough for feature-length films and high-definition videoconferencing.

Interface advances are a bit trickier. Screen resolution, brightness, and contrast will improve, but size will remain an inherent problem of mobile computing. Our pockets aren't getting any bigger. Here we must look to more exotic solutions like digital paper, head-mounted displays, and web on the wall. It's tough to predict when and whether these technologies will shift from prototype to product. For now, visibility is limited. Similar challenges exist with input. Fat fingers on tiny keyboards are a major obstacle to mobile productivity. Chorded keyboards like the Twiddler, shown in Figure 4-1, are unlikely to enjoy widespread adoption despite the efforts of wearable computing advocates.* And, voice recognition has gone nearly nowhere in over a decade, thanks to inter- and intrapersonal variation (we don't even speak consistently ourselves) and disruptive background noise.

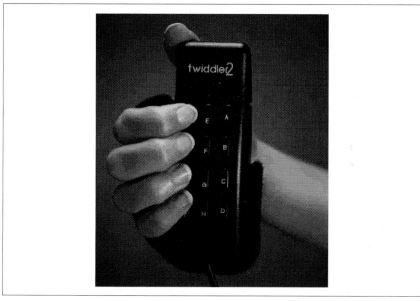

Figure 4-1. The Twiddler 2 is a four ounce combination keyboard and mouse manufactured by the Handkey Corporation

Even major breakthroughs in speech-to-text software won't remove all the problems. Do you really want strangers listening to you write email? Speaking of which, we must also acknowledge the limits of attention. Can we truly focus on reading and writing while walking and talking? Can we be entirely productive in taxi cabs and noisy cafés? Inveterate multitaskers will answer yes. Others will argue they've no choice, and for many globe trotters and road warriors, this is true. But many of us will find that much of our work is still best performed in a safe, familiar office environment with an ergonomic keyboard, a mouse, and a big flat panel monitor. In other words, smartphones will not replace desktops and laptops, but their use will expand into a growing number of growing niches. We may use them everywhere, but not for everything. We may rely on them for ready reference, but not so much for research. Just because we can doesn't mean we will.

---

* Georgia Tech professor Thad Starner invented a four-inch strip of Velcro that sticks a Twiddler to a shoulder bag, enabling conversion from storage to use in two seconds, the optimal speed of access based upon his usability research. Are you ready for geek chic?

What's most exciting is the anticipation of unforeseen applications. In the *Cluetrain Manifesto*, David Weinberger notes, "We don't know what the Web is for but we've adopted it faster than any technology since fire."[*] At the crossroads of pervasive computing and the Internet, this sentiment only rings louder. Adam Greenfield, a pioneer of everyware and a passionate advocate for ethical ubicomp notes:

> Ubicomp is here right now. It lives on your cellphone, or in a chip on your dashboard, and comes out to play anytime you turn down iTunes' volume with your phone or cruise through an EZPass lane.
>
> It is also, and simultaneously, what Gene Becker calls 'a hundred-year problem': a technical, social, ethical and political challenge of extraordinary subtlety and difficulty, resistant to comprehensive solution in anything like the near term.[†]

Visions of pervasive computing and ambient findability ignite our imaginations, but we're a far cry from best practices for everyware, and the road ahead is neither straight nor narrow. But we should not fear this journey for we will not walk alone. As we wander the wilderness of ubicomp, our mobile devices will be our lifeline, connecting us as never before: indivisible and intertwingled. Can you hear me now?

Wayfinding 2.0

Speaking of journeys, it should come as no surprise that wayfinding is among the most fertile soils for technologies of intertwinglement. For even as we advance into a connected century, we continue to spend great scads of time moving our physical bodies through space, and despite the ready availability of maps and street signs, we still manage to get ourselves lost. Lost in cities or inside buildings or on the way.

One of my more memorable experiences happened a couple of years ago on the way to the doctor's office. You see, our youngest daughter was born with an underdeveloped tear duct system that failed to properly drain the lubricants of her eyes. She would often wake in the morning with one or both eyes sealed shut with guck (that's the technical term). Blocked tear ducts are a common problem in infants, but fortunately 90% of cases resolve themselves. Unfortunately, Claudia was in the 10% that require surgical probing, an outpatient procedure in which a blunt metal wire is inserted

---

[*] *The Cluetrain Manifesto* by Rick Levine, Christopher Locke, Doc Searls, and David Weinberger. Perseus (2000), p. 43.

[†] "Design Engaged: The Final Programme" by Adam Greenfield. From *http://v-2.org/displayArticle. php?article_num=908.*

through the tear duct while the child lies wrapped in a blanket screaming bloody murder.

Suffice it to say, my wife and I were not very happy as we piled into the minivan and headed for our visit with the pediatric ophthalmologist. And after 20 minutes of trying to reconcile our map, shown in Figure 4-2, with the territory, we were considerably less happy. So, we're late. We're lost. Claudia is presciently crying in the back seat. My wife is trying to decode the worse than useless map. And I'm calling the doctor's office on my cell phone to ask for directions while our minivan swerves violently through city streets.

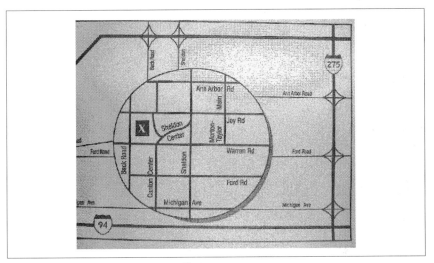

Figure 4-2. The map to the doctor's office

This is the gritty reality of transmedia wayfinding at the dawn of the 21st century. Concrete mazes rendered barely navigable by the combination of lousy maps, illegible signs, missing landmarks, and desperate phone calls. Perhaps I exaggerate, but only to make an important point. Wayfinding remains an inefficient and even dangerous activity. At best, we waste time and endure needless stress. At worst, lives are lost when distracted drivers intertwingle their cars with immovable objects. There must be a better way, and fortunately we appear poised on the brink of breakthrough. After eons of bumbling around the planet, we're about to take navigation to a whole new level. Wayfinding 2.0. And it begins with location awareness.

The crown jewel of next-generation wayfinding is the Global Positioning System (GPS), a satellite-based radionavigation system that enables land, sea, and airborne users to determine their three-dimensional position (latitude, longitude, altitude) and velocity from anywhere at any time. Compliments of the U.S. Department of Defense, 24 satellites orbiting 20,200 kilometers above the earth provide us with location awareness, accurate to within three meters. Equipped with a GPS receiver and map database, we can find our way like never before. In-car navigation systems like Hertz NeverLost, shown in Figure 4-3, are among the earliest mainstream applications. Select your destination from pre-programmed points of interest or enter an address or intersection, and they provide voice and visual turn-by-turn directions. These navigation systems are becoming increasingly accurate and affordable, and will eventually become user-friendly.

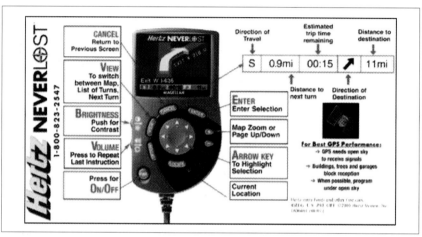

Figure 4-3. The Hertz NeverLost navigation system

Our kids will wonder how we ever survived without them, and not just in the car. GPS receivers grow smaller and more ubiquitous every year. Handheld units are increasingly common for hiking in natural and urban environments. Many runners now chart their course and track mileage using a GPS watch, like that in Figure 4-4. And a variety of GPS attachments are available for smartphones. I'm expecting my next Treo will come with embedded GPS. No more printed maps. No more getting lost on the way to the doctor.

Of course, GPS isn't perfect. It doesn't actually work everywhere. Buildings, terrain, electronic interference, and sometimes even dense foliage can block signal reception. And for certain applications, such as wayfinding inside buildings, three meter accuracy isn't sufficient. For extreme ubiquity and precision, we will rely (like sea turtles and honeybees) on a composite of positioning approaches. Outdoors, receivers that combine GPS with complementary dead-reckoning technologies to estimate position by continuously tracking course, direction, and speed can handle the big picture.

Figure 4-4. The Garmin Forerunner 201 GPS watch

Indoors, and for any application in which extreme precision is required, we will depend on the location-sensing capabilities of other radiofrequency (RF) technologies such as Wi-Fi, Bluetooth, Ultra-wideband, and RFID. UWB, for example, is not just a standard for fast wireless communication. It just so happens that by calculating relative distances between nodes, UWB can achieve fine spatial resolution, identifying location to within one inch.

Location-Sensing Techniques

Despite the profusion of technologies, patents, standards, and acronyms, there are only three major location-sensing techniques.[a]

Triangulation. Performed by *lateration* (the use of multiple distance measurements between known points) or *angulation* (the measurement of angle or bearing relative to points with known separation).

Proximity. Measuring the nearness of an object to a known set of points.

Scene analysis. Uses features of a scene observed from a vantage point to assess the location of the observer or objects. Features may consist of visual images, electromagnetic sensing, or other measurable physical phenomena.

[a] "Location Systems for Ubiquitous Computing" by Jeffrey Hightower and Gaetano Borriello. Available at *http://www.intel-research.net/Publications/Seattle/062120021154_45.pdf*.

In considering potential applications of location-sensing technologies, it's important to recognize a few important distinctions beyond range and accuracy. First, there's the difference between physical position and symbolic location. GPS provides physical position such as 47°39'17" N by 122°18'23" W at a 20.5 meter elevation. A separate database or geographic information system is required to convert physical positions into symbolic locations such as in the kitchen, on the ninth floor, in Ann Arbor, next to a mailbox, or on an airplane approaching Amsterdam. Today's crude databases and flat map interfaces are insufficient for modeling the complexity of 3D urban environments.

Similarly, there's the distinction between absolute and relative location. GPS receivers use latitude, longitude, and altitude to define a shared reference grid (absolute position) for all located objects. In relative systems, on the other hand, each object has its own frame of reference. For example, a receiver used in a mountain rescue effort indicates the relative location (direction and proximity) of an avalanche victim's transceiver.

Finally, there are issues of recognition and privacy. Systems that perform localized location computation ensure privacy. In GPS, the receiving device computes its own position, and the satellites have no knowledge about who uses their signals. In contrast, active badge and RFID systems require the located object to self-identify so that position may be computed by the external infrastructure. In other words, navigation and surveillance can intertwingle. Technology architecture has social impact.

But let's not wallow in privacy paranoia just yet. Why not dwell for a moment on the bright side of the big picture? The experience of becoming lost involuntarily is headed towards extinction. And our newfangled networked appliances promise all sorts of fascinating applications. Even before the widespread use of location-sensing technologies, wayfinding is being transformed by the Web. MapQuest and Google Maps provide coast-to-coast coverage, delivering maps and step-by-step driving directions to our computers and mobile phones. Google Local and Yahoo! Local enable the quick lookup of nearby businesses and services. Simply enter an address, city, or Zip Code to find a coffee shop, restaurant, movie theater, gas station, museum, or dentist near you. In merry old England, even the ancient tradition of wayfinding while intoxicated has been revolutionized by the Web, where countless web sites provide detailed maps for pub crawls of varying levels of difficulty. Pub crawl generators, like the one shown in Figure 4-5, make recommendations based on postal code, desired number of pubs, and the maximum distance between each pub.

And on a more sober note, before visiting a hospital, shopping mall, or subway, we can grab a map from the web site, like that in Figure 4-6, and plan our trip from start to finish. Some bed and breakfasts even provide photos of each room, so we can see (and select) destinations from our point of origin. This brings new meaning to the experience of déjà vu.

Researchers have begun to intertwingle these applications with location-aware devices. At IBM's Almaden Research Laboratory, for instance,

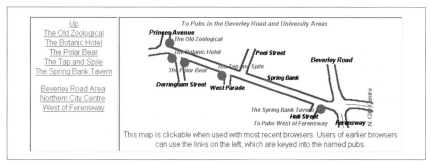

Figure 4-5. A virtual pub crawl in Hull, England; http://www.eyorks.com/hullpub/

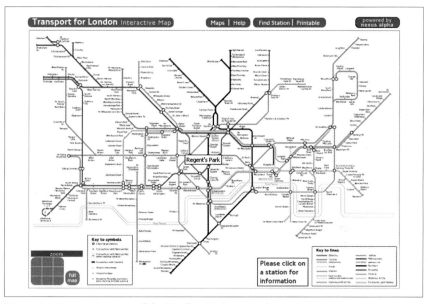

Figure 4-6. Interactive map of the London Underground

J.C. Spohrer has advanced the notion of geocoding through the World-Board infrastructure:

> What if we could put information in places? More precisely, what if we could associate relevant information with a place and perceive the information as if it were really there? WorldBoard is a vision of doing just that on a planetary scale and as a natural part of everyday life. For example, imagine being able to enter an airport and see a virtual red carpet leading you right to your gate, look at the ground and see property lines or underground buried cables, walk along a nature trail and see virtual signs near plants and rocks, or simply look at the night sky and see the outlines of the constellations.[*]

---

[*] "Information in Places" by J.C. Spohrer. Available at *http://www.research.ibm.com/journal/sj/384/spohrer.pdf*.

We're still a head-mounted display away from fulfilling this vision of augmented reality in a mainstream sense. The technologies exist, but the costs remain prohibitive, for now. But that's not stopping us from transforming our world into a vast planetary chalkboard by annotating physical locations with virtual notes and images. These memes have long since escaped the laboratory and can be seen playing in the wild and on the Web.

For instance, the Degree Confluence Project is collecting photographs and stories from all of the latitude and longitude integer degree intersections in the world: precise places in space, tagged with images and text, as shown in Figure 4-7. Anybody with a GPS receiver and a digital camera can contribute. Thus far, the collection boasts 40,000 photographs from 159 countries. So what is the purpose of this global database of images? Well, the stated goals include creating an organized sampling of the world and documenting the changes to these locations over time. But deep down, it's about experimentation and fun. It's about using technology to rediscover our natural world. In the words of one seeker:

> One thing that I like a lot about confluence hunting is that this is a place that you have never seen (and many times will never see again), that you know exactly where it is, you do not how to get there but will find a way and, no matter how it turns out to be you will be so glad and satisfied to have been there!*

A similar adventurous spirit infuses the sport of geocaching, a high-tech treasure hunting game for GPS users. In this game, people set up caches of maps, books, CDs, videos, pictures, money, jewelry, tickets, antiques, and other treasures. They then post the location coordinates on the Internet, and participants try to find the caches. The challenge derives from the distinction between knowing the location and reaching the location. Caches have been hidden on mountains, in trees, and even underwater. On any given day, *geocaching.com* lists over 100,000 caches in hundreds of countries.

And, in anticipation of GPS-enhanced photography, Mappr, shown in Figure 4-8, is already tapping into the wealth of descriptive metadata supplied by Flickr users to match pictures to places. For now, Mappr's reliance on the uncontrolled, imprecise vocabulary of free tagging results in unreliable geographic data, but the maps sure are cool.

These games spread like wildfire because they capture the imagination. They are harbingers of a new relationship with physical space. It's still early for mainstream applications, so we play our way into the future. That said, serious uses are beginning to take shape. The BrailleNote GPS, pitched as the

* The Degree Confluence Project, *http://www.confluence.org/*.

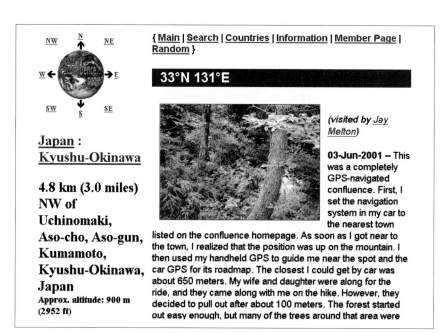

NW N NE

W ← confluence → E

SW ↓ SE
   S

33°N 131°E

Japan :
Kyushu-Okinawa

4.8 km (3.0 miles)
NW of
Uchinomaki,
Aso-cho, Aso-gun,
Kumamoto,
Kyushu-Okinawa,
Japan
Approx. altitude: 900 m
(2952 ft)

(visited by Jay Melton)

03-Jun-2001 -- This was a completely GPS-navigated confluence. First, I set the navigation system in my car to the nearest town listed on the confluence homepage. As soon as I got near to the town, I realized that the position was up on the mountain. I then used my handheld GPS to guide me near the spot and the car GPS for its roadmap. The closest I could get by car was about 650 meters. My wife and daughter were along for the ride, and they came along with me on the hike. However, they decided to pull out after about 100 meters. The forest started out easy enough, but many of the trees around that area were

Figure 4-7. A confluence in Japan; http://www.confluence.org

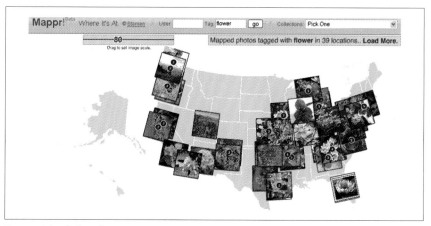

Figure 4-8. Flickr's flowers on Mappr's map

"Cadillac of Wayfinding Systems," enables people who are blind or visually impaired to more easily navigate unfamiliar areas. Drawing upon a massive points-of-interest database, blind pedestrians can locate a train station or bus stop, meet a friend for lunch at a new restaurant, or find their way back to a hotel. Independence through ubicomp. And in Europe, a smartphone software provider named Psiloc sells an application for defining location-based actions and events. Sleep-deprived commuters can set an alarm to wake them when their train approaches the station, even if it's ahead of schedule. If desired, an SMS message will automatically alert colleagues of your impending arrival. You can even use the Periodic SMS feature to provide family members with regular updates on your location. And all of a sudden, for better or for worse, we've once again dropped through the looking glass, for the same technology that helps us avoid getting lost can also help us be found.

Findable Objects

My favorite artifact from the future is the Wherify Wireless GPS Personal Locator for Kids, shown in Figure 4-9. It's a watch, clock, pager, and tracking device all in one. You can buy it on Amazon. It's available in Galactic Blue and Cosmic Purple. With a special key fob, you lock it on your kid's wrist. And then, from the comfort of your home or office, you track your child's location via the Internet, as shown in Figure 4-10. Features include:

- Choose from a standard street map or custom aerial photo.
- Define preset times for automatic "locates."
- Use "breadcrumbs" to see travel routes and location history.
- Unlock the locator remotely once your child arrives safely at soccer practice.

Is this the greatest product ever or what? As Wherify explains, "Now you can have peace of mind 24 hours a day while your child is the high tech envy of the neighborhood!"

Of course, knowing *where they are* and knowing *what they're doing* are very different things. The latter will require video and audio surveillance. Don't worry. That's coming.

Are you freaking out yet? Do you find this product disturbing in a profound Orwellian sense? Or, are you on the other side of the fence? Do you see it as yet another miracle of modern convenience? Perhaps you're already on Amazon, placing your order.

That's what I love about this product. It forces us to think about how we *want* to use technology. As parents, we go to great lengths to protect our kids. In an imperfect world, we use the available raw materials to craft solutions that work for our families. One size does not fit all, as illustrated by this amusing confession of George Brett:

> My folks used a chicken wire pen for me. Sounds bad, but then again we lived near a large lake and my older cousins wanted me to join them swim-

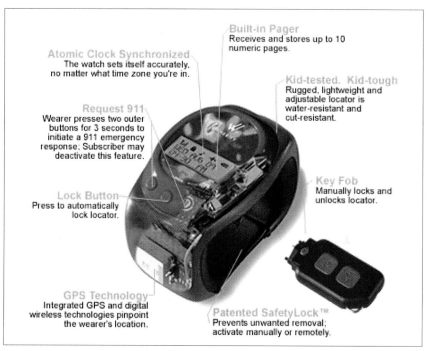

Figure 4-9. The GPS Locator for Children from Wherify Wireless

Figure 4-10. The custom aerial view

ming—so they were locked out and I was locked in. Other side benefit is that the alligators couldn't get me either.*

We've been improvising in this fashion for millennia, making tough decisions that balance freedom and privacy with safety. But never before have we had so much choice. For when it comes to toddler tracking, the diversity of technologies and applications is amazing. Invisible perimeters or "geofences" alert you if your child leaves the house or yard or campsite. Radiofrequency leashes sound the alarm if they wander too far in a shopping mall or at the beach: you set the "safe distance" from 15 to 75 feet. And if visiting an amusement park, why buy when you can rent? At Legoland in Denmark, parents can pay three euros to have their child tagged for the day. The locator, attached by disposable wristband, lets the park's 2.5 million square foot Wi-Fi network track the child anywhere in Legoland. Since approximately 1,600 children are separated from their parents in Legoland each year, this promises to be a seriously useful service.

Personal locator devices are also used to help care for people with Alzheimer's disease, a progressive, irreversible condition that robs victims of their memory, cognitive abilities, and social skills. Alzheimer's patients tend to lose track of time and become disoriented, so wandering can be a huge problem:

> Between 60 to 70 percent of all patients with Alzheimer's will wander, and possibly get lost, at some point during the course of their disease. Of these, a staggering 50 percent will die if they are not found within 24 hours.†

Applied Digital Solutions sells a device called the Digital Angel, which is worn as a watch and comes with a clip-on pager. Using GPS mapping software and cell phone networks, the Digital Angel alerts caretakers by email (sent to a cell phone, computer, PDA, or text pager) when a patient has wandered out of a designated area.

This intertwingling of GPS with cellular communication is an increasingly popular tracking solution. It is the foundation of vehicle location and management systems such as OnStar and Networkcar.‡ GPS-enabled cell phones are used by law enforcement agencies to keep track of officers, and by parents to monitor the location and velocity of their teenage children:

---

* Comment by George Brett during a discussion on Ed Vielmetti's Vacuum mailing list.

† "GPS Technology and Alzheimer's Disease," *http://alzheimers.upmc.com/GPS.htm.*

‡ GM's OnStar pioneered the concept of smart cars with GPS and cellular communications to support wayfinding, remote diagnostics, emergency services, and stolen vehicle recovery. Networkcar's innovation has been to eliminate the need for professional dispatchers by placing the information directly into the consumers' hands via the Web. Companies (such as trucking firms and car rental agencies) can monitor their vehicle fleets. Individuals can monitor their own cars.

As her daughter enjoyed a weekend road trip, Donna Butler sat back home 120 miles away at her personal computer and watched a blue dot tick slowly across the screen. But not slowly enough. 'They were going 85 on the interstate where the speed limit is 70,' said Butler, who interrupted Danielle's getaway to let her know, 'I will personally come up there and drive you home."

And if you don't want someone to know they're being watched, a wide variety of covert tracking devices are sold at web sites like *spyville.com*. One "satisfied" customer explained, "My husband was saying he was working late and it turned out he was going to the Holiday Inn. Now he's living at the Holiday Inn." These devices are also used for high-tech stalking. In a recent case, a man who attached one under his estranged wife's car was ordered by a judge to wear a GPS device himself as part of his sentence for felony menacing by stalking: a punishment to fit the crime.

So, which of these location-sensing applications are acceptable? Some can be lifesavers while others are just plain spooky. Stalking clearly crosses the line. But what about tracking your teenager? Is that okay? Should you inform them of their status as findable object? Legally, you can track without telling, but you'll have to work out the ethics yourself.[†] These are decisions we'll have to make as individuals, corporations, and societies. And before we have time to decide, our relationships to findable objects are going to get a whole lot weirder thanks to the wonders of radiofrequency identification.

RFID is a disruptive technology poised to shift paradigms by transforming our ability to identify and locate physical objects. Initially, RFID is being sold as a next-generation barcode system on steroids that enables real-time supply chain visibility. Major retailers such as Wal-Mart and Tesco are in the midst of high-profile RFID rollouts designed to streamline logistics, reduce costs, stop theft, and improve demand forecasting accuracy. Key advantages of RFID over traditional barcode systems include:

- RFID tags can be read from a distance through walls, packaging, clothes, and wallets. There is no requirement for *line of sight* between label and reader.

- With barcodes, every can of Coke has the same universal product code (UPC). With RFID, each can has its own unique ID number. It's classified as a can of Coke but also identified as a *unique individual object*.

- RFID spills beyond identification into positioning. The same radiofrequency technologies that support communication (e.g., Wi-Fi, UWB) also enable the precise location and *tracking* of tagged objects.

---

* "Cell Phones Ring Knell on Privacy." *Chicago Tribune*, January 1, 2005.
† "Tracking Your Children With GPS: Do You Have the Right?" by Stephen N. Roberts. Available at *http://wireless.sys-con.com/read/41433.htm*.

It is this combination of advantages that compels RFID to migrate far beyond the supply chain. Consider this astonishing hodgepodge of applications:

- Pharmaceutical companies are using RFID to provide track-and-trace protection for drugs and reduce drug counterfeiting and thefts. Each 100-tablet bottle of OxyContin, a widely abused pain killer, is now tagged by the manufacturer.
- Hotels have deployed wireless RFID-enabled mini-bar systems to track their Toblerones, Pringles, and $5 Cokes. Remove any item for more than 30 seconds and the e-fridge chalks up a sale and notifies the hotel's central database.
- Electronic toll collection systems such as E-ZPass rely on RFID to identify moving vehicles and charge the associated accounts.
- The European Central Bank is reportedly embedding RFID tags in euro notes to cut down on counterfeiting and money laundering.
- Delta and United Airlines are actively exploring RFID baggage tracking programs to eliminate the errors and delays that plague the current system.
- For more than a decade, pets have been injected with RFID tags. Estimates put the number of RFID-enabled recoveries in the U.S. and Canada at 5,000 per month. In Portugal, under a government initiative to control rabies, all two million dogs must be implanted with radio tags and registered in a national database by 2007.
- Hospitals are using RFID bracelets to keep track of doctors, nurses, and patients. The same technology is used in prisons to track prisoners and in schools to track students.
- At the Baja Beach Club in Barcelona, patrons with subdermal RFID implants can access the VIP lounge and pay for drinks without needing to carry a wallet or cash.
- In a bid to fight government corruption, Mexico's attorney general and several key staff members had RFID chips implanted to support tracking and authentication.

Clearly, radiofrequency identification is not your grandfather's barcode. RFID represents a big step towards ambient findability. We're talking about an Internet of Things without precedence in human history. Products, possessions, pets, and people all rendered into findable objects: cataloged, searchable, and locatable in space and time. The future exists today, and we're just waiting for the world to catch up. As Adam Greenfield notes:

It is a future structurally latent in the new schema for Internet Protocol addressing, IPv6, which, with its 128-bit address space, provides some 6.5 x 10^{23} addresses for every square meter on the surface of our planet, and therefore quite abundantly enough for every pen and stamp and book and door in the world to talk to each other.[*]

But before we presume the ability to find anyone or anything from anywhere at any time, it's worth evaluating the limits of today's technology. After all, RFID is subject to the familiar tradeoffs of size, range, power, and cost. Weakness in a single area can rule out a whole suite of potential applications. To understand these tradeoffs, it's important to distinguish between active and passive RFID. While both technologies use radiofrequency energy to communicate between the tag and reader, the method of powering the tags is different.

Passive tags have no internal power source. They depend on signals from the reader for activation. In passive systems, the tags are small and cheap, but the readers are expensive, their range is constrained to roughly three meters, and they're unable to read multiple tags at once. This limits passive tag systems to scenarios in which tagged items move past readers (through a doorway or along a conveyor belt) in single file: great for supermarket checkout but mostly useless for nonlinear applications beyond the supply chain. In other words, you shouldn't worry about Victoria's Secret tracking your underwear, unless you're being tailed by a suspicious operative wielding a bulky RFID reader.

Active tags, on the other hand, rely on internal batteries to continuously power their communication circuitry. With active RFID, the tags aren't as small or cheap, but the systems can track thousands of items moving at more than 100 mph with operating ranges of 100 meters or more.[†] Additionally, active tags can support read/write data storage, thereby enabling a hospital wristband or badge to store a patient's complete, editable medical record. So, active tags have some great advantages, but they're too costly for most retail applications, and too big for many covert operations. For now, you wouldn't want a subdermal active tag implant. It would be quite lumpy and changing the battery could be a real pain in the neck or arm or wherever. In any case, you get the picture. When it comes to ambient findability, RFID is as much promise as product.

---

[*] "All Watched Over by Machines of Loving Grace" by Adam Greenfield. Available at *http://www.boxesandarrows.com/archives/all_watched_over_by_machines_of_loving_grace.php.*

[†] "Active and Passive RFID: Two Distinct, But Complementary Technologies for Real-Time Supply Chain Visibility," *http://www.autoid.org/2002_Documents/sc31_wg4/docs_501-520/520_18000-7_WhitePaper.pdf.*

But, it would be a shame to allow these due diligence findings to obscure our foresight and dim our curiosity. These barriers will not stand. The future that exists today will spread and mutate like a virus into tomorrow. Location-aware mobile computing devices. Ubiquitous high-speed radiofrequency networks. Active tags that are smaller, cheaper, and more abundant than postage stamps. We will have the technology. But how will we use it? To find our missing keys, socks, and remote controls? To locate our pets, kids, and spouses? To track our own movements through space and time? What small apparent oddities of today are destined to become commonplace? This question is asked and answered by science-fiction author and futurist Bruce Sterling, who describes a new class of self-revealing, user-configurable objects called spimes:

> The most important thing to know about spimes is that they are precisely located in space and time. They have histories. They are recorded, tracked, inventoried, and always associated with a story. Spimes have identities, they are protagonists of a documented process. They are searchable, like Google.[*]

Sterling notes that books are well on their way to becoming spimes, for a book on Amazon is far more than the words between its covers. We can learn its cost and publisher; what other books the author has written; what readers think about the book; what other books those readers have bought; and we can keyword search the full text. Data and metadata intertwingle with patterns of purchase and use:

> When you shop for Amazon, you're already adding value to everything you look at on an Amazon screen. You don't get paid for it, but your shopping is unpaid work for them. Imagine this blown to huge proportions and attached to all your physical possessions. Whenever you use a spime, you're rubbing up against everybody else who has that same kind of spime. A spime is a users group first, and a physical object second.[†]

How will we handle that leap from class of product to individual object? The possibilities are intriguing. Let me Google my own bookcase. Show me all the books my friends own and where they're located. Figure 4-11 shows one implementation. Does anybody in my neighborhood have this book? Where are they right now? But these imaginings also invoke questions about metadata and trust. What (and who) will we tag, and with whom will we share that information?

Already mobile social software services such as AT&T's Find People Nearby are moving beyond the binary presence management of instant messaging by

---

[*] "When Blobjects Rule the Earth" by Bruce Sterling. SIGGRAPH 2004 Keynote. Available from *http://www.boingboing.net/images/blobjects.htm.*

[†] Sterling, *http://www.boingboing.net/images/blobjects.htm.*

Figure 4-11. Delicious Library, a personal, networked, location-aware, multimedia, personal lending library that exists today

enabling us to share our location within trusted networks of friends, family members, and colleagues. Participants are learning to manage the intricacies of their own privacy. How much detail should we divulge? Will we store and share our location history, as Joi Ito has done in Figure 4-12? And when do we choose to be totally *unfindable*?

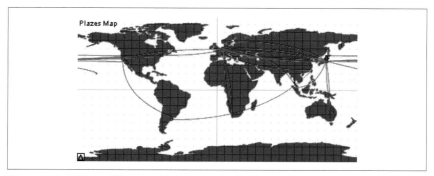

Figure 4-12. Joi Ito, a blogger and venture capitalist uses IndyJunior maps on top of Plazes data to chart and publish his travels

Conversely, we must define acceptable levels of metadata awareness. How much do we really want to know about the locations of our acquaintances? How wide are our circles, socially and spatially? Open the gates too wide and we'll drown in sociospatial metadata, victims of virtual claustrophobia. And as we turn our products, possessions, pets, physical objects, and places into spime, we risk information overload and metadata madness. How will we choose the right tags? How will we find what we need? Location is easy, but what about aboutness? Can the folksonomies of Flickr and del.icio.us survive in the wild? Will free tagging deliver a physical world of findable objects, or will we find ourselves lost in the chaos of spime synonymy? This is the paradox of ambient findability. As information volume increases, our ability to find any particular item decreases. How will we Google our way through a trillion objects in motion? We're staring down the barrel of the biggest vocabulary control challenge imaginable, and we can't stop adding powder.

Imports

At the soft edges of cyberspace, we're importing vast amounts of information about the real world while simultaneously designing new interfaces for export. It is this great intertwingling of physical and digital that promises a radical departure from the present, for we're talking about nothing less than adding eyes and ears to our digital nervous system. The amount of information on today's Web is insignificant in relation to the oceans of data that will pour into cyberspace through a global network of sensory devices. Change won't come overnight, but our children will inherit a different world.

I stole a glimpse at this future a few years ago through the eyes of our eldest daughter, Claire. It was Christmas break, and I finally had a chance to play with my new laptop and wireless network while concurrently entertaining Claire. In the spirit of "embracing the genius of the AND," I decided to try out some webcams, eventually settling on the Live Earthcam at Times Square, shown in Figure 4-13. So, I'm sitting on the couch in Ann Arbor with our two year old, and we're streaming a real-time video feed from New York City, and she loves it! Traffic lights orchestrate an ebb and flow of people and cars, while honking horns punctuate the constant buzz of the big city. For some time, Claire and I are simultaneously in Ann Arbor and New York. This is not the willing suspension of disbelief. It's not like television or the movies. We are experiencing real places in real time. The people are not actors. There is no script. Claire is fascinated by the bright yellow cars, and I explain they are "taxi cabs" and they help people get from place to place. When one appears on screen, she yells "taxi cab, taxi cab." And this experience is seamlessly transferred into the real world where cries of "taxi cab, taxi cab" ring out on trips to the grocery store for the next several years. And each time this occurs, I'm struck by the oddity of a lesson learned at home through a virtual window onto Times Square.

A different yet related event occurred in Ann Arbor the following year. A new Blockbuster Video opened less than a mile from our home, and within months of the grand opening, the manager was found brutally murdered inside her own store. We were horrified and worried, particularly since the police had no immediate suspects. Fortunately, the crime was solved within

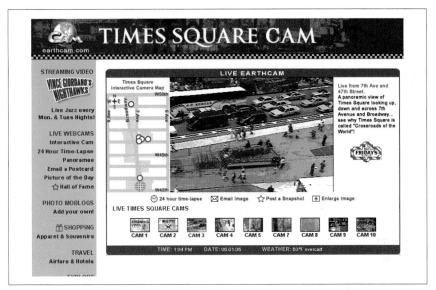

Figure 4-13. Times Square via Live Earthcam

days, thanks to a surveillance video camera located *across the street* which had captured on tape a disgruntled employee entering Blockbuster at the time of the crime. It was the "across the street" part that caught my attention. I hadn't realized the ubiquity and power of surveillance technology, until then.

The strange connection between these two stories is, of course, the video camera, which every year grows smaller, cheaper, more powerful, and better networked. From the fun of webcams to the gravity of telemedicine and remote surgery, the camera connects us to distant places and people. Yet it also raises serious concerns about the fate of privacy in a world of nanny cams and ceiling bubbles.

> In 1998, the New York Civil Liberties Union issued a report detailing the prevalence of surveillance cameras in New York City and found 2,397 government and private cameras on the streets of Manhattan. In recent years, however, particularly after 9/11, we have seen these numbers grow exponentially. For example, in one of the more alarming cases, NYCLU volunteers found 13 video surveillance cameras in Chinatown in 1998; a similar search in 2004 found more than 600 such cameras.[*]

And these are only the visible, outdoor cameras that volunteers were able to identify by wandering the streets. Who knows how many hidden cameras

---

[*] Surveillance Camera Project, *http://www.nyclu.org/surveillance_camera_main.html*.

populate the homes, businesses, parking lots, and roads we pass through each day? Not that nighttime is any real obstacle, for infrared cameras provide the ability to see clearly for thousands of feet in total darkness. And then there are those *eyes in the sky* we call satellites. Constellations of spacecraft hurtling through space, hundreds or thousands of miles above our planet, taking snapshots at sub-meter resolution. We have one of these snapshots hanging on the wall in our living room. It's a picture of our neighborhood taken from space. Our house is clearly visible, and upon close examination, you can pick out the Japanese Zelkova tree we planted in our front yard a few years back. These images can be personal and powerful. They provide a new way to see our world at its best and worst, as Figure 4-14 illustrates.

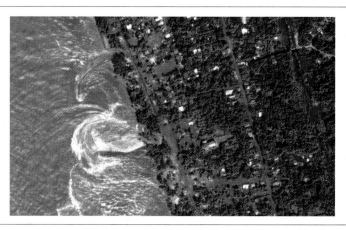

Figure 4-14. Kalatura, Sri Lanka. Receding waters from tsunami (image from DigitalGlobe's QuickBird satellite, December 26, 2004. © 2005 DigitalGlobe Services, Inc.)

Of course, eyes work even better when aided by ears, and this potent combination is now being used to stem gun violence on the streets of Chicago and Los Angeles. SENTRI employs microphone surveillance to recognize the sound of a gunshot. The system can precisely locate the point of origin, turn a camera to center the shooter in the viewfinder, and make a 911 call to summon the police.* The key innovation of SENTRI is its ability to distinguish a gunshot from other loud noises typical in an urban environment. In fact, this type of automatic *pattern recognition* is critical in a world where the flow of data far exceeds the limits of human attention. We can't possibly watch all the video or view all the satellite imagery, so we must rely on

---

* "Waiting for the Gun" by Eric Mankin. From *http://www.usc.edu/uscnews/stories/10810.html*.

computers to identify the important events and patterns, converting physical data into symbolic information. This is an area of active research and development, as the following examples illustrate:

- In Microsoft's Easy Living project, real-time 3D cameras provide stereovision positioning capabilities. These vision location systems can identify individuals by analyzing combinations of silhouette, skin color, and face pattern.

- In Georgia Tech's Smart Floor, embedded sensors capture footfalls. By utilizing biometric features such as weight, gait distance, and gait period, these smart floors are able to identify and track individuals by their unique footfall signatures.

- Sensors are increasingly used in homes and businesses and by law enforcement agencies to detect chemical and biological agents in our air and water.

- Sensors that track velocity, force, and location are finding their way into baseball gloves, football helmets, and soccer balls. Hockey pucks are loaded with infrared sensors that enable television viewers to see 95 mph slap shots as streaking comets.

- In many cities, networks of video cameras, radar devices, and road-embedded sensors provide commuters with real-time, online information about accidents, construction, road conditions, and traffic speeds, like the map in Figure 4-15.

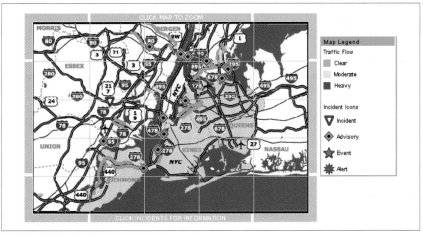

Figure 4-15. Traffic conditions in New York from TrafficPulse at http://www.traffic.com/

And here's one of my favorites. An English company is developing a health-care toilet with embedded sensors that can monitor your diet and detect health problems:

> The sensors can analyse for diabetes, for instance. Blood sugar can be monitored and the results sent via the Internet to the user's doctor or pharmacist.*

Physical output becomes digital input in this transformation of waste into metadata. Sensors are coming to a loo near you. And this strange business of sensory cyberspace imports has just begun. We can hardly imagine all the weird and wonderful possibilities.

Exports

We will experience a growing trade deficit with cyberspace as we deposit far more data than we can ever withdraw, but that's not to say that exports won't be equally fascinating as we design new interfaces to networked information. After all, the future of interface is not just about huge flat panel monitors and tiny PDA screens. It's about listening to your car navigation system. It's about reading the *New York Times* on e-paper. And if David Rose has his way, it's about feeling your email. Let me explain.

I first met David Rose in 2002 at the AIGA Experience Design Summit held at the Bellagio Hotel in Las Vegas. David is founder and chief creative officer of an MIT startup called Ambient Devices. At the conference, he captured our attention with a brilliant show-and-tell featuring a colorful array of products and prototypes. First up was a beautiful frosted glass orb that slowly transitions between thousands of colors to show changes in the weather, traffic, or the health of your stock portfolio, shown in Figure 4-16. Simply plug the orb into a power outlet, and it's instantly up and running on a nationwide wireless network. Then, visit Ambient's web portal to customize your orb. You can even track news, pollen forecasts, and the presence of colleagues on Instant Messenger. Designed to leverage the cognitive psychology phenomenon of pre-attentive processing, this crystal ball delivers glanceable, back-channel information. This is calm computing at its best.

But David didn't stop with the orb. He had a whole table full of groovy gadgets, including an inbox-connectable pinwheel that spins faster and faster as your messages pile up (until the hurricane force compels you to check email) and a web-configurable health watch to remind people when to take their

---

* Twyford Bathrooms, *http://www.twyfordbathrooms.com/*.

Figure 4-16. The Ambient Orb

prescription medicines. It didn't take long for us to appreciate the full potential:

> Ambient's vision is to embed information representation in everyday objects: lights, pens, watches, walls, and wearables. With Ambient, the physical environment becomes an interface to digital information rendered as subtle changes in form, movement, sound, color or light.*

And if these ideas intrigue you, it's definitely worth taking a short trip upstream to the MIT Media Laboratory and the Tangible Media Group of Hiroshi Ishii.

> Tangible Bits, our vision of Human Computer Interaction (HCI), seeks to realize seamless interfaces between humans, digital information, and the physical environment by giving physical form to digital information and computation, making bits directly manipulable and perceptible. The goal is to blur the boundary between our bodies and cyberspace and to turn the architectural space into an interface.†

Hiroshi's group has created a whole slew of exhibits and prototypes to illustrate the possibilities of tangible user interfaces. They include:

Bricks
Graspable user interfaces that allow direct control of virtual objects through physical handles called "bricks."

Lumitouch
A pair of interactive, Internet-enabled picture frames for emotional communication. When a user touches their frame, the other's frame lights up.

MusicBottles
Three corked bottles that serve as containers and controls for the sounds of the violin, the cello, and the piano, shown in Figure 4-17.

---

* Ambient Devices, *http://www.ambientdevices.com/*.
† Tangible Media Group at MIT, *http://tangible.media.mit.edu/*.

Figure 4-17. MusicBottles from the MIT Media Lab

Unfortunately, it's hard to convey the rich, dynamic, interactive nature of tangible bits through print media. Direct experience is ideal, but the project videos available at *http://tangible.media.mit.edu/* are the next best substitute.

Meanwhile, not so far away physically or philosophically, Jeffrey Huang at Harvard's Graduate School of Design has been exploring the intersection of the Internet and architecture. As a proof of concept in "convergent architecture," Huang worked with the architect Muriel Waldvogel to build the Swisshouse, a new type of consulate that connects a geographically dispersed scientific community. Persistent audio-video linkages and "web on the wall" are among the innovations used to build a bridge between academic institutions in the greater Boston area and a network of universities in Switzerland. The physical building serves as a large interface for knowledge exchange and as a testbed for studying telepresence, remote brainstorming, and distance learning.

In *Digital Ground*, University of Michigan professor Malcolm McCullough explores the emerging relationships between physical and digital architectures:

> The built environment organizes flows of people, resources, and ideas. Social infrastructure has long involved architecture, but has also more recently included network computing. The latter tends to augment rather than replace the former; architecture has acquired a digital layer.*

---

* *Digital Ground* by Malcolm McCullough. MIT Press (2004), p. 47.

At this point of intersection, McCullough believes the study of how people deal with technology and how people deal with each other through technology will be central to success, noting "as a consequence of pervasive computing, interaction design is poised to become one of the main liberal arts of the twenty-first century."

Convergence

Of course, the ultimate convergence will happen even closer to home as the human body becomes an environment for computers. The first big step in this corporal merger is wearable computing, an area of active research at many of the world's leading universities. Steve Mann, a pioneer in the field, has been working on WearComp for more than 20 years, with results shown in Figure 4-18. It now looks like his dedication is about to pay off. Wearable computing is disappearing into the fabric of life, becoming ubiquitous and invisible.

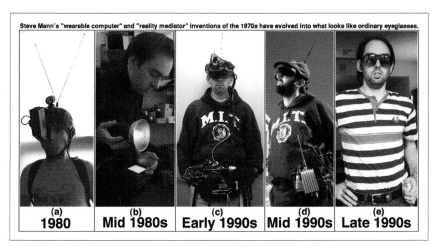

Figure 4-18. The evolution of Steve Mann's wearable computer

For instance, Xybernaut's wearable computing platform is already being used by aircraft mechanics and engineers at Federal Express, Boeing, and the U.S. Department of Defense to dramatically improve mobile worker productivity. And in the consumer realm, Motorola recently announced a deal with Oakley to create wearable wireless glasses (to be used in combination with cell phones and MP3 players) and a separate venture with Burton to build Bluetooth-enabled jackets and headgear for skiers and snowboarders.

Motorola's vision is to enable "seamlessly mobile wireless communications anywhere and everywhere consumers want to be."* One example from Philips is shown in Figure 4-19.

No Kidding... Designed to give parents peace of mind, this children's garment uses mobile phone, fabric antennas, radio tagging and camera technology to monitor and pinpoint their kids' position. To the children, however, the coat is a device that they can use to play exciting outdoor games. The series of games use characters with identity chips attached to the respective garments. On the screen on the jacket sleeve, the child sees the character that represents another child, and as the children move around, their "characters" can be seen moving on the screen.

Figure 4-19. New Nomads by Philips

Beyond the ability to check email while skiing down a mountain, one of the more interesting applications of WearComp is the capture of life experiences. In the MyLifeBits project, a team at Microsoft is exploring the mix of hardware, software, and metadata tags necessary to store and retrieve everything we see, hear, and read. Based on success with wearable prototypes that integrate cameras, sensors, and terabyte hard drives, the researchers predict that "users will eventually be able to keep every document they read, every picture they view, all the audio they hear, and a good portion of what they see." They expect terabyte drives to be common and inexpensive (<$300) by 2007. In addition to serving as digital scrapbooks and photo albums, these wearables will provide memory augmentation, helping us recall the name of the person we just met. This idea of personal video capture is nothing new to Steve Mann who "built the world's first covert fully functional WearComp with display and camera concealed in ordinary eyeglasses in 1995." His vision of inverse surveillance has recently taken on new life under

---

* "Motorola, Oakley Team to Make Wearable Wireless" by Keith Regan. *E-Commerce Times*, January 21, 2005.

the label of *sousveillance*, which means in French "to watch from below." In a backlash against government and corporate surveillance, growing numbers of citizens are donning wearables to watch the watchers, a trend toward the "reciprocal transparency" that David Brin explores in *The Transparent Society.*[*]

But we shouldn't get too hung up on wearable computing, which is really only a stepping stone on the path to cybernetic transformation. Despite our uneasy relationship with such terms as "cyborg" and "transhuman," the convergence of mechanical, electronic, and biological systems is well underway. For instance, Stephen Hawking has a progressive neurodegenerative disease called ALS that has rendered him physically unable to walk or talk. And yet, he is able to live a productive and rewarding life as a husband, father, and preeminent physicist. He does so with the help of a customized wheelchair with an onboard laptop with cellular and wireless devices, a universally programmable infrared remote control for opening doors and operating consumer electronics, a speech synthesizer, and a handheld input device with one button. It is this single button and the equipment behind it that connects Stephen Hawking to his family, his colleagues, and the global Internet. With respect to his personal experience and his contributions to society, man and machine have been intertwingled. And he is not alone. Consider the following:

- About 78% of Americans have had an amalgam of copper, silver, and mercury permanently implanted in their bodies. We call them fillings.

- More than 60,000 people worldwide have had cochlear implants surgically embedded to compensate for damaged or non-working parts of the inner ear.

- In 2004, the U.S. Food and Drug Administration approved the country's first radiofrequency identification chip for implantation into patients in hospitals. The intent is to provide immediate positive identification. The tags are injected into the fatty tissue of the upper arm. Their estimated life is 20 years.

- A company in Israel has developed an ingestible "camera-in-a-pill" which obtains color video of the gastrointestinal tract as it passes through the body. And Mini Mitter in the U.S. sells a core body temperature monitor that features ingestible capsules that communicate wirelessly with the outside world.

- New video games with wireless headsets allow players to control the action with their brain waves. And scientists at Duke University have built a brain implant that lets monkeys control a robotic arm via the Internet with their thoughts.

---

[*] *The Transparent Society* by David Brin. Perseus (1998).

In the realm of implants and ingestibles, fact is stranger than fiction. We've already stepped onto the slippery slope of corporal convergence. As technology relentlessly increases the angle of inclination, direction can be assumed, while distance and velocity remain in question. Healthcare supplies the wedge for early adoption. Who wants to fight against lifesaving technologies? Fun and fashion will carry them from hospital to high school, as ringtones and belly rings intertwingle themselves into the bodies of teenagers. The conspicuous consumption of cybernetics will drive parents crazy, though it will be what's hidden that keeps us up at night. But eventually, we'll reach a techno-cultural tipping point, and convergence will go mainstream. Will we be chipped at birth? Will it become illegal to live implant-free? How far will we go? Only time will tell. Our destination lies shrouded in fog, but our direction is clear. We're on the yellow brick road to ambient findability, and we've got magic slippers to help us find our way.

Asylum

Do we really want to go there? This is a question we must continue to ask as we intertwingle ourselves into a future with exciting benefits but cloudy costs. Though subdermal RFID chips were approved on the basis of their lifesaving potential, the FDA raised serious questions about their safety including electrical hazards, MRI incompatibility, adverse tissue reaction, and migration of the implanted transponder. In their guidance document, the FDA also detailed the risks of compromised information security, noting that transmissions of medical and financial data could be intercepted, and that the devices could be used to track an individual's movements and location. I don't know about you, but I plan to wait out the beta test.

But even as we spurn the bleeding edge, these technologies seep into every nook and cranny of our lives. I recently stumbled across a telling story about ubiquitous computing at a leading psychiatric hospital in Manhattan.[*] Based on the belief that allowing patients to talk on the phone may speed their recovery from depression or hasten their emergence from psychosis, doctors had approved the use of cell phones and other wireless devices. The patients loved this new freedom, and the ward was soon bustling with cell phones, laptops, Palm Pilots, and BlackBerries. As you might suspect, the results were mixed. The enhanced personal communication appeared to have real clinical benefit for many patients, but on the other hand, nurses found themselves constantly recharging batteries. In a place where people may use

---

[*] "In a Mental Institute, the Call of the Outside" by David Hellerstein, M.D. *New York Times*, January 27, 2004.

power cords to hang themselves, wireless has special meaning. However, the most serious problem was disruption. As one doctor noted:

> There was a constant ringing on the unit. All these different ring tones. Some people would put them on vibrate mode and sneak them into group and then want to walk out to answer their calls. Or they would be talking to their friends and would ignore the nurses.

The final straw was the new camera phones, which threatened to eliminate any semblance of privacy. The intertwingling of inside and outside had spiraled out of control. The very essence of the asylum as a save haven and protective shelter was under attack. The decision was made. Laptops and Palm Pilots were permitted, but no more cell phones. At first, there were protests as patients argued their right to communicate, but eventually the right to privacy and the virtues of peaceful sanctuary prevailed. Of course, as the lines between cell phones and Palm Pilots blur, the debate may be revisited. Said one doctor:

> Is it over? I don't know. Here at the institute, our enthusiasm for wireless connectivity has been tempered by reality. We have reclaimed a fragment of asylum. But my guess is that we will face a next challenge by the wireless world, and that we will continually have to work to define our relation to it. My guess is that the battle has just begun.

This story resonates in the outside world. We love our cell phones but not the disruption. We love our email but not the spam. Our enthusiasm for ubiquitous computing will undoubtedly be tempered by reality. Our future will be at least as messy as our present. But we will muddle through as usual, satisficing under conditions of bounded rationality. And if we are lucky, and if we make good decisions about how to intertwingle our lives with technology, perhaps we too can reclaim a fragment of asylum.

CHAPTER 5
Push and Pull

Be still like a mountain and
flow like a great river.
—Lao Tzu

What do bananas, text books, and beach sand have in common? No, it's not a joke, though the answer dwells in the borderlands between humor and horror. We're talking about ambient advertising, and it's funny and fascinating, until it crosses *the line*.

Originally known as fringe, buzz, stealth, or guerilla marketing, ambient advertising has gone mainstream. Specialty agencies such as Ambient Planet and Diabolical Liberties are helping to spread the word into every nook and cranny imaginable. Beer mats, bar toilets, pizza boxes, receipts, floors, cars, parks, and prescription pharmacy bags. Ads lurking in the holes on golf courses. Commercials carved in sand. Logos inscribed on foreheads. Everyday objects and nature itself are becoming channels for push media.

But where is *the line*? At what point is push too pushy? Our emotions lure us toward the extreme. For instance, I hate spam. It invades my inbox, steals my attention, and wastes my time. It's bad for me, and I'm pretty sure it's bad for society. Some days, I get angry and search for solutions in the shady bazaar of black lists, white lists, filtering algorithms, and challenge-response systems. But mostly, I try to ignore it, control-deleting my way ahead in a state of learned helplessness. Spam is the poster child for the dark side of push.

Spam is also a canned meat product and the subject of a hilarious Monty Python sketch in which two customers try to order a spam-free breakfast from a menu that includes it in every entrée. The waitress tries to help by noting "Well, there's spam, egg, sausage, and spam, that's not got *much* spam in it," while a raucous gang of Vikings repeatedly sings "Spam, Spam,

Spam, Spam, Lovely Spam, Wonderful Spam," louder and louder, until the song reaches an ear-shattering operatic climax. Interestingly, Spam was one of the few meats excluded from the British food rationing during World War II, and the British became seriously sick of it, hence the skit. And eventually, the phenomenon of marketers flooding Usenet newsgroups and email inboxes with junk advertising messages was named spamming in honor of this sketch. Or at least that's what I learned after a Google search landed me on the *Spam (Monty Python)* page of the Wikipedia.

Which is why I love the Web. How could I not love a medium that puts the full text of this sketch and a streaming audio version of the Vikings' spam song at my fingertips? Heck, I can even nip over to NetFlix and pull Volume 8 of "Monty Python's Flying Circus" all the way to my mailbox in Ann Arbor. The Web allows me to pull what I want into my attention or my possession when I want it. No more shopping malls or pushy sales clerks. Books, clothes, groceries, movies, musical instruments, and 30 HP Nortrac Bulldozers are just a few clicks away. The sky's the limit.

But there I go again. Rushing to the extremes when the action is in the middle. For while I must confess a penchant for pull, I would never wish for a world without push. I would shed no tear for the loss of telemarketing or door-to-door soliciting. But no more advertising? No more unsolicited advice? The idea of a push-free world reminds me of my visit to the anechoic (echo-free) chamber at Consumers Union. The walls sport massive fiberglass wedges that prevent reverberation. The floor is formed by a platform suspended above the bottom by wires. And to nullify external noise, the entire room is encased in a meter of cement. This is the ultimate quiet room, perfect for testing stereo systems and speakers. It sounds like a wonderful place to escape the cacophony of modern life, but alone in this room, you find the silence is deafening. And that's how I imagine a world without push. In the absence of push, we lose our inspiration for pull.

Like yin and yang, shown in Figure 5-1, push and pull are interdependent opposites that cannot exist alone. Each contains the seed of its opposite. They flow into one another, constantly evolving, continuously seeking balance. Though we may be inclined to cleave them into distinct categories of black and white, good and evil, hot and cold, or active and passive, the truth lies where they meet. In the words of Lao Tzu, the Chinese philosopher and librarian best known as the father of Taoism, "to see things in the seed, that is genius."[*]

---

[*] According to legend, Lao Tzu was appointed Keeper of the Imperial Archives in 6th century B.C. by the King of Zhou. His studies of the archive's books led to the insights that inspired Taoism, a philosophy and religion dedicated to seeking "the way" or "the path."

Figure 5-1. The tai-chi symbol unites yin and yang

Consider, for instance, the XML-based "really simple syndication" format of RSS, which allows us to subscribe to news feeds, blogs, event calendars, search results, and any other type of dynamic web content. We can now turn the sources we find into services that find us. We can selectively *opt in* to push, so we need not remember (or take the time) to pull.

Of course, when we subscribe to blog feeds and email discussion lists, we assume the cost of noise in return for the value of signal. We ignore most posts. Only a few engage our attention. But we're used to filtering push. We do it all the time when we "listen" to our colleagues. We remember only the juiciest gossip and most relevant word of mouth.

The genius of yin-yang is also evident in the success of Google. By intertwingling the world's greatest search engine with tasteful, targeted advertisements, Google struck a balance between push and pull that sent their stock into the stratosphere. Google's brand of sponsored search, which clearly differentiates paid ads from results, is one of those bright ideas that seems obvious in hindsight, but few appreciated in advance.

Not so long ago, huge flows of money chased after directories and portals, dismissing search as a dog with fleas. *Wired* magazine forecast the demise of web browsers at the hands of personalized push technologies such as Point-Cast. Online advertisers went intrusive, spawning multitudes of winking, blinking banner ads, pop-ups, pop-unders, interstitials, eyeblasters, and sky-scrapers. And competitors like MSN Search blended paid ads with results, earning income at the expense of trust.

Eventually, Google's strategy of balance proved itself friendly to users and advertisers, and the rest, as they say, is history. But that's not to say the Web has entered a new era of enlightened marketing. Far from it. Today's Web is littered with obnoxious, ineffective ads. Marketing departments fight (and often win) the battle for screen real estate. Home pages are seen as channels for delivering messages and persuading users. A generation of marketing professionals, raised in the glory days of broadcast television, struggles to adapt to the new medium. We see it every day. Push at the expense of pull. The balance remains out of kilter, and the web design community is lured toward the opposing extreme. Marketing is demonized and ridiculed in countless books, cartoons, blogs, and discussion lists. In Dilbert, for instance, the Pointy-Haired Boss's son, who hid in an attic for four years instead of attending college, was hired by the company and made VP of Marketing due to his complete lack of knowledge.

As the user experience designer Peter Merholz points out:

> Because so much marketing *is* bad, and so many marketers *are* clueless, there's a tendency to dismiss marketing altogether.

And yet, as Merholz implicitly suggests, design and marketing are not ene-mies. On the contrary, they are inextricably bound together. It is impossible to find the line where one ends and the other begins. And in this ambiguity lies opportunity. Design and marketing professionals would do well to learn from one another. It's time to forsake the tyranny of the OR and embrace the genius of the AND.*

Marketing

At the peak of the dot-com boom, the authors of *The Cluetrain Manifesto* took center stage with their passionate cry for the end of business as usual. With scathing wit, they dissected and discredited mass marketing as a nasty industrial age hangover. The book hit the bestseller lists, and the authors were promptly lifted onto pedestals. Then the bubble burst and their revolu-tionary call to arms suddenly seemed out of place, quickly forgotten amid

---

* *Built to Last: Successful Habits of Visionary Companies* by James Collins and Jerry Porras. HarperCollins (1997).

the rubble. This is unfortunate because the manifesto's message still rings true:

> A few thousand years ago there was a marketplace. Never mind where. Traders returned from far seas with spices, silks, and precious, magical stones. Caravans arrived across burning deserts bringing dates and figs, snakes, parrots, monkeys, strange music, stranger tales. The marketplace was the heart of the city, the kernel, the hub, the *omphalos*. Like past and future, it stood at a crossroads. People woke early and went there for coffee and vegetables, eggs and wine, for pots and carpets, rings and necklaces, for toys and sweets, for love, for rope, for soap, for wagons and carts, for bleating goats and evil-tempered camels. They went there to look and listen and to marvel, to buy and be amused. But mostly they went to meet each other. And to talk.[*]

Markets are conversations. Or at least they were until the holy trinity of mass production, mass marketing, and mass media derailed the discussion. And in the swirl of cultural, economic, and technological change that surrounds the Internet, the conversations have begun once more. But many have forgotten how to listen. Herein lies both problem and opportunity. Markets are changing faster than marketing professionals. This results in terrible channel noise as old messages are pushed through new media with increasing intensity and desperation. But for those who are willing to listen and learn, today's marketplace offers opportunities for interaction, insight, and innovation unseen since the ancient bazaars of spices, silks, and magical stones.

Marketing Defined

The process of planning and executing the conception, pricing, promotion, and distribution of ideas, goods, and services to create exchanges that satisfy individual and organizational goals.

—American Marketing Association

Marketing is a societal process by which individuals and groups obtain what they need and want through creating, offering, and freely exchanging products and services of value with others.

—Philip Kotler, Marketing Management

So what are these changes? How is the new economy different from the old economy? Well, for starters, today's consumer enjoys more:

---

[*] *The Cluetrain Manifesto* by Rick Levine, Christopher Locke, Doc Searls, and David Weinberger. Perseus (2001), p.9–10.

Buying power

The Internet (and online services like Priceline, Orbitz, and Froogle) have shifted the balance of power from business to consumer by dramatically increasing our ability to compare competitor prices and product attributes.

Variety

The selection of goods and services at our fingertips is remarkable. Amazon alone boasts several million distinct items in its product catalog. No physical store can match this. And we can shop internationally without leaving our homes.

Information

From *Consumer Reports* and *Epinions* to discussion lists and blogs, our access to product evaluations and reviews is unprecedented. Greater knowledge and transparency brings a welcome shift in emphasis from packaging to quality.

Of course, as Herbert Simon noted, this wealth of information brings a corresponding poverty of attention. So many channels. So many choices. And from the perspective of marketing, so much competition! Equilibrium has been punctuated. Marketing has entered a period of high-speed evolution. Emergent species include one-to-one marketing, permission marketing, viral marketing, cross-merchandising, product placement, ambient advertising, and spam. Only the fittest will survive.

And in today's attention economy, fitness requires a new balance between push and pull. The playing field has shifted, and yet few companies understand the new rules. In their bias towards push, marketing is missing opportunities to make products more findable. Those of us in design see this every day. We advocate more user research. We argue for better search and navigation, fewer banner ads, and cleaner code. Let's make it easier for our customers to find what they need when they need it. But marketing doesn't listen. Perhaps we need to speak louder, or plaster our message on a few million bananas.

Design

Design has emerged as one of the world's most powerful forces. Our lives are intimately touched by architectural, environmental, industrial, and visual design. Most of the places and objects that shape our experience have been designed by intention. And the Internet has created new frontiers for interaction, information, and communication design.

Know Thy Customer

The power of pull has always been appreciated by the best minds in business. As the legendary management guru Peter Drucker explains:

> There will always, one can assume, be need for some selling. But the aim of marketing is to make selling superfluous. The aim of marketing is to know and understand the customer so well that the product or service fits him and sells itself. Ideally, marketing should result in a customer who is ready to buy. All that should be needed then is to make the product or service available.

> —*Management: Tasks, Responsibilities, Practices* by Peter Drucker. Harper & Row (1973), p. 64–65

In the past decade, an eclectic community of pioneers embraced the challenges of web design. Graphic designers, information architects, web producers: our titles are as diverse as our skills, and yet we face the same challenges. We must understand our medium and our users. We must keep pace with the relentless march of technology. And we must communicate our value and defend our designs over and over again. When dealing with marketing folks in particular, we find ourselves repeating the following mantra:

You are not the user.

The emergence of usability, user-centered design, and user experience design testifies to the value of user research. "You don't know your user" is a common corollary, required when explaining that focus groups don't provide the same insight into user behavior as field studies, search logs, and usability testing.

The experience is the brand.

While perhaps an exaggeration, we're trying to swing the pendulum from a preoccupation with image to an appreciation of experience. No matter how pretty the logo, if users can't find what they need, the brand is damaged.

You can't control the experience.

The user holds the steering wheel and will surprise you at every turn. She may ignore your headlines. She may never visit your home page. And she might be using a smart phone with the images turned off.

The debates often begin in the tug of war over home page real estate. Marketing sees the home page as a channel for positioning, promotion, and persuasion. The page overflows with logos, tag lines, photographs, brand messages, banners, and special offers, as Figure 5-2 illustrates. Search and navigation are granted a few pixels to the side, the sum total of user needs and corporate information captured in a handful of words and a query box.

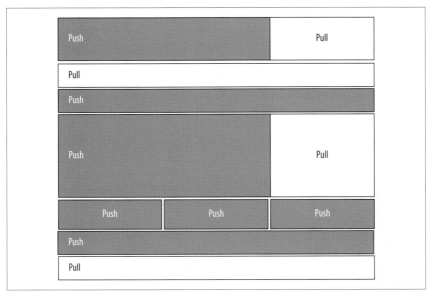

Figure 5-2. A typical pushy home page

And yet, from years of research, we appreciate the immense difficulty of representing collections of content and objects with labels and keywords, as Figure 5-3 attempts. We know that even by bubbling up a few sample subcategory labels, we can dramatically enhance the scent of information. But to do that, we need more real estate. And so we must explain, educate, evangelize, and advocate. We must push for pull. It's our professional responsibility. Reaching the balance in Figure 5-4 isn't easy.

Figure 5-3. Categories and sample subcategories at Yahoo!

Figure 5-4. A better balance between push and pull

Of course, the experience doesn't begin or end with the home page. Users often start by plugging a keyword or two into Google. Ranking and presentation in the result set impacts brand perception before users even enter the site. In Figure 5-5, who would you rather be: Harvard or Stanford? Or how about Columbia, sitting in obscurity beneath the fold? Users assign most authority and credibility to the top results, and the descriptions that appear may determine whether they decide to visit in the first place.

And for many who do visit, the home page is nothing more than a signpost, hastily scanned and quickly forgotten on the way to somewhere else. Visitors want products, support, data, documents, and downloads. They're not interested in our message. The only time they really notice our site is when they become lost or stuck. And it's at that very point when push is most annoying. I'm desperate for help and you're pitching an upgrade? I know what I want. How about a navigation system that lets me find it?

Finally, as designers and user advocates, we must consider the myriad variables affecting presentation, such as bandwidth, screen size, resolution, and browser type. As increasing numbers of people access our sites with mobile devices, we must get better at bridging the gap between desktops and handhelds. At 175K, Duke's heavyweight home page (pictured in Figure 5-6) is definitely not worth the 51 second wait on my Treo.

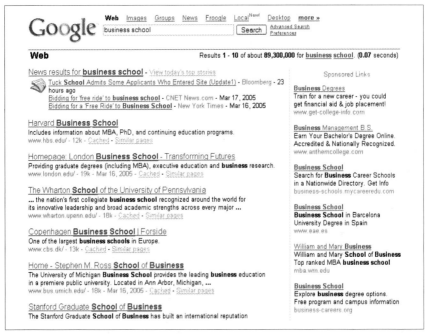

Figure 5-5. Business schools ranked by Google

Figure 5-6. The Fuqua School of Business on a Treo

Neither is Frontier Airlines, shown in Figure 5-7, which weighs in at 272K and requires almost two minutes to load. Ironically, these home pages don't look particularly good in any browser. This is not about a tradeoff between aesthetics and accessibility. It's about bad design.

In contrast, Google's 4K pages, shown in Figure 5-8, load within 10 seconds and still look sexy through the eyes of a Treo. Tastes great. Less filling. The duality of tai chi. The genius of the AND.

Figure 5-7. Frontier Airlines on a Treo

Figure 5-8. Google search results on a Treo

This is the philosophy that led me to create the user experience honeycomb, shown in Figure 5-9.* We cannot be trapped in a zero sum game that pits usability against marketing.

Figure 5-9. The user experience honeycomb in Japan

Instead, we should acknowledge the rich, dynamic, interconnected blend of qualities that shape the user experience. For instance:

---

* First published in a Semantics article by Peter Morville called "User Experience Design" (June 2004). Available at *http://semanticstudios.com/publications/semantics/000029.php*.

Useful

As practitioners, we can't be content to paint within the lines drawn by managers. We must have the courage and creativity to ask whether our products and systems are useful, and to apply our deep knowledge of craft and medium to define innovative solutions that are more useful.

Usable

Ease of use remains vital, and yet the interface-centered methods and perspectives of human-computer interaction do not address all dimensions of web design. In short, usability is necessary but not sufficient.

Desirable

Our quest for efficiency must be tempered by an appreciation for the power and value of image, identity, brand, and other elements of emotional design.

Findable

We must strive to design navigable web sites and locatable objects, so users can find what they need.

Accessible

Just as our buildings have elevators and ramps, our web sites should be accessible to people with disabilities (more than 10% of the population). Today, it's good business and the ethical thing to do. Eventually, it will become the law. Standards-based design for accessibility also supports access via mobile devices.

Credible

Thanks to some ground-breaking research out of Stanford's Persuasive Technologies Lab, we're beginning to understand the design elements that influence whether users trust and believe what we tell them.

Valuable

Finally, it's not just about the user. Our sites must deliver value to our sponsors. For nonprofits, the user experience must advance the mission. With for-profits, it must contribute to the bottom line and improve customer satisfaction.

The honeycomb hits the sweet spot by serving several purposes at once. First, it's a great tool for advancing the conversation beyond usability. More opening move than endgame, it gets people talking about qualities absent from the diagram and catalyzes discussion about goals and priorities. Is it more important to be desirable or accessible? How about usable or credible? In truth, it depends on the site's unique mix of context, content, and users, and any tradeoffs are better made explicitly than unconsciously.

Second, this model supports a modular approach to design. Let's say you want to improve your site but lack the budget, time, or stomach for a complete overhaul. Why not try a targeted redesign, perhaps starting with the "Stanford Guidelines for Web Credibility" as a resource for evaluating and enhancing the credibility of your web site.[*]

Third, each facet of the user experience honeycomb can serve as a singular looking glass, transforming how we see what we do, and enabling us to explore beyond conventional boundaries. For example, I realized some time ago that while "information architect" describes my profession, findability defines my passion.

Of course, while there's value in examining these facets in isolation, it's also vital to understand the surprising ways they interact. In fact, after a decade of focus on defining the individual elements, many of the Web's leading experts have now begun to spend time in the areas of intersection and overlap.

For instance, in *Emotional Design*, usability guru Don Norman provides solid evidence that attractive things work better, citing the surprising results of research studies in which "usability and aesthetics *were not expected* to correlate."[†] But they did, again and again, in scientifically repeatable fashion. Similarly, research led by B.J. Fogg at the Stanford Persuasive Technology Lab has shown a powerful link between credibility and desirability.[‡] Users trust web sites that are well designed. They also trust sites that appear at the top of search results, further proof of a link between credibility and findability.

And in *Speed Up Your Site*, Andy King connects the dots between file size, the psychology of flow, and the user experience, noting that the *bailout rate* or "percentage of users who leave a page before it loads" jumps from 6% at 34K to 30% at 40K.[§] King cites numerous studies that demonstrate the negative impact of slow-loading web pages on perceived usability, credibility, findability, and even content quality.

And then there's Jeff Veen, who loves to raise eyebrows by claiming "I don't care about accessibility," and then explaining that "when Web design is practiced as a craft, and not a consolation, accessibility comes for free."[**] And, Jeffrey Zeldman, who teaches that designing with web standards not

---

[*] "Stanford Guidelines for Web Credibility," *http://www.webcredibility.org/guidelines/*.

[†] *Emotional Design* by Don Norman. Basic Books (2004), p. 18.

[‡] Stanford Web Credibility Project, *http://credibility.stanford.edu/*.

[§] *Speed Up Your Site* by Andrew B. King. New Riders (2003), p. 17.

[**] "I Don't Care About Accessibility" by Jeff Veen. From *http://www.veen.com/jeff/archives/000503.html*.

only improves accessibility for people with disabilities but also for people with handhelds.* By separating structure, presentation, and behavior into independent yet interrelated layers, we can simultaneously improve usability, accessibility, desirability, findability, interoperability, and forward compatibility, while reducing costs and schedules. The genius of the AND. In their own way, each of these gurus speaks of simplicity, interdependence, and balance. Much like Lao Tzu.

Findability Hacks

So, enough with balance already. While I admit findability is not the only important element of the user experience, I'm not ready to concede its primacy online. I'm sure we can all agree with the basic truth expressed by this ancient proverb:

> Findability Precedes Usability
>
> In the Alphabet and on the Web
>
> You Can't Use What You Can't Find

Seriously, findability is one of the most thorny problems in web design. This is due in part to the inherent ambiguity of semantics and structure. We label and categorize things in so many ways that retrieval is difficult at best. But that's only the half of it. The most formidable challenges stem from its cross-functional, interdisciplinary nature. Findability defies classification. It flows across the borders between design, engineering, and marketing. Everybody is responsible, and so we run the risk that nobody is accountable.

In fact, in most organizations, findability falls through the cracks. Web site search engines return lousy results because designers and engineers don't collaborate to fine-tune the relevance ranking algorithms. Dazzling product catalogs wallow in obscurity because marketing and engineering can't work together on search engine optimization. And navigation systems fall short because information architects and brand architects fail to map marketing jargon to the vocabulary of users. Time after time, findability falls through the cracks between roles and responsibilities, and everybody loses.

For all these reasons, findability merits special attention. At the enterprise level, we must find ways to cultivate cross-functional collaboration. And at the individual level, we must have the curiosity and courage to wander beyond the safety of our job titles into unmapped, interdisciplinary territory. In the spirit of the hack, in the positive rather than pejorative sense,

---

* *Designing with Web Standards* by Jeffrey Zeldman. New Riders (2003).

findability invites clever solutions to interesting problems. Hackers don't worry so much about org charts. They just get the job done. In this sense, we need more findability hackers who are willing to roll up their sleeves and get their hands dirty.

For instance, many professionals in the design community have maintained an unhealthy distance from the practice of search engine marketing, which includes search engine advertising (SEA) and search engine optimization (SEO). We view SEO as too technical and write off SEA as marketing's responsibility. And we keep the whole topic at arms length to avoid being tainted by association with unethical search engine marketing practices such as cloaking, keyword stuffing, and domain spamming. And yet, this field offers huge opportunities for us to connect our users with the content they seek. SEO, in particular, is interwoven with usability, information architecture, copywriting, and other elements of the user experience. As the SEO expert Shari Thurow notes:

> One of the most important components of a successful search engine marketing campaign is the link component, also referred to as site architecture. Site architecture refers to a web site navigation scheme, individual page layout, and how directories are set up on your web server. Site architecture is very important because the search engine spiders must be able to find and record the keyword-rich text on your web pages.[*]

In fact, we must give credit to the pioneers of search engine marketing for taking a practical, cross-disciplinary approach to web findability and turning it into a multi-billion dollar industry in less than a decade. Leading firms, such as iProspect, have made a compelling case for return on investment in findability, citing statistics such as:

- Second only to email, the most popular activity for U.S. Internet users is search—an estimated 40% of them are using the Web to make product or service purchases.

- Consumers are five times more likely to purchase products or services after finding a web site through a search engine than through a banner advertisement.

- Over half of all Internet users never go past the first two pages of search results.

And these firms haven't let functional or disciplinary boundaries get in the way of solving problems for customers and users. Just consider the following SEO guidelines:

---

[*] *Search Engine Visibility* by Shari Thurow. New Riders (2002), p. 89.

- Determine the most common keywords and phrases (with optimal conversion rates) that users from your target audience are entering into search engines.

- Include those keywords and phrases in your visible body text, navigation links, page headers and titles, metadata tags, and alternative text for graphic images.

- Proceed cautiously (or not at all) when considering the use of drop-down menus, image maps, frames, dynamic URLs, JavaScript, DHTML, Flash, and other coding approaches that may prevent a search engine spider from crawling your pages.

- Create direct links from your home page, sitemap, and navigation system to important destination pages to increase their page popularity ranking.

- Use RSS feeds with ample backlinks to your site's target destinations to encourage subscriptions and visits and boost organic search rankings.

- Reduce HTML code bloat and overall file size by embracing web standards to ensure accessibility and improve keyword density.

SEO can certainly be viewed as part of marketing. Information search is a key component of the consumer buying process. Marketing textbooks, using the models in Figures 5-10 and 5-11, describe the opportunity represented by an "aroused consumer" engaged in an "active information search."[*]

Figure 5-10. Five stage model of the consumer buying process (adapted from Kotler, p. 204)

As marketing guru Philip Kotler notes, "a company must strategize to get its brand into the prospect's awareness set, consideration set, and choice set."[†]

And yet, to view SEO as the sole purview of marketing is a huge mistake. For starters, design and engineering must be involved in the work anyway, since much of the optimization (such as editing content and code) cannot be easily outsourced.

But it's more than that. Connecting users with the content and services we design and build is part of our broader mission. It's not good enough to

---

[*] *Marketing Management* by Philip Kotler. Prentice Hall (2002), p. 204.
[†] Kotler, p. 205.

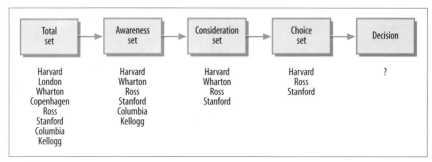

Figure 5-11. *The consumer decision making process (adapted from Kotler, p. 205)*

create a great product and expect someone else to worry about how people will find it. Together with form and function, findability is a required element of good design and engineering. I relentlessly make this case to government agencies and nonprofits that don't have marketing departments. They tend to shy away from SEO as overly commercial, but they're missing a great opportunity to fulfill their mission by helping people find what they need.

Also, while search engine optimization is obviously an important factor in defining the first step into a consumer's awareness set, findability plays a role in each and every step, from problem recognition to purchase decision to post-purchase behavior. Findability does not fit neatly inside boxes. Findability is more about connecting the boxes.

But perhaps we're expecting too much by asking people to cross functional and disciplinary boundaries in such entrepreneurial fashion. We may ultimately need to fill the findability gap by editing the org chart, as a few pioneers have already done. For instance, at Telecom New Zealand, a daring information architect named Michael Williams decided that "findability engineer" better described his role and made the case for a change. This was initially regarded by HR as a "very irregular job title," but Michael was persuasive, and the new title was eventually conferred. According to his manager, Sally Myles, this change has generated positive results, including:

- It's a conversation starter and creates the opportunity to explain the relationships between information architecture, search, usability, and personalization.
- It has raised Michael's profile within the organization as the findability expert.
- It reminds the team that our overall goal is to help our users find what they need.

Hewlett-Packard has taken findability a step further by defining a "Findability Group" that includes an interdisciplinary team responsible for user interface design, information architecture, and search, thereby creating a vital bridge across vertical silos. Perhaps we will see more findability engineers and findability teams in the coming years.

Of course, companies that create a "Department of Findabilty" will run the risk of building yet another vertical silo when they should be using findability to get horizontal. What we really need is more informed, findability-aware participants in the existing roles within design, engineering, and marketing. Now, that would be a big step forward.

As HP co-founder David Packard famously remarked "Marketing is far too important to be left only to the marketing department." In my opinion, so is findability. But we race ahead of reality. For now, findability is in the hands of daring individuals with a cross-disciplinary approach to problem solving. For now, findability is just an elegant hack.[*]

Personalization

So far, we've focused on active, directed seeking, empowering users to find what they want when they want it. But findability isn't limited to pull. Findability is also concerned with how information and objects find us. What factors influence our exposure to new products, people, and ideas? AdWords algorithms, one-to-one marketing, intelligent agents, email alerts, collaborative filtering, contextual advertising: what tools can we use to turn the tables on findable objects? How do we bring the mountain to Mohammed?

We are talking, of course, about personalization, a strange hybrid of push and pull that dwells in the borderlands between marketing and technology. The promise of personalization is simple: by modeling the behavior, needs, and preferences of an individual, we can serve up customized, targeted content and services. The benefits to the user are clear. No more searching. Information comes to you. Web, email, instant messenger, mail, phone, fax: select the best channel, define your interests, and you're set. And the value proposition for marketing is even greater. Targeted advertising, customized messaging, differential pricing, and product personalization offer huge opportunities to cut costs, boost sales, and improve customer satisfaction and loyalty.

Unfortunately, it's not that easy. In fact, personalization is exceedingly difficult. Yes, there are notable exceptions. In cases where our needs are simple

---

[*] Adapted from Christina Wodtke, who said, "Information architecture is just an elegant hack."

to describe (or derive) and relatively unchanging, personalization works well. The Weather Channel serves up forecasts based on our Zip Code. Yahoo! uses our profile to deliver custom sports scores and stock prices. Google Alerts lets us track the occurrence of keywords in news stories and web sites. Amazon remembers our name, address, and credit card information, and provides incredible access to our own account information and transaction history.

But beyond these shallow waters, there be dragons. In recent history, companies have poured vast amounts of time and money into technologies that promise to anticipate individual interest with respect to products or knowledge, and most of these efforts have failed for a variety of reasons, which include:

The ambiguity of language
> An abundance of synonyms and antonyms in our language forces the same messy tradeoffs between precision and recall for personalization that we encounter in information retrieval.

The paradox of the active user
> It takes time to complete a profile that specifies interest with any reasonable precision. Few users will have the patience to set these parameters in advance even if they would save time overall.

The ambiguity of behavior
> Does everyone who purchases catnip have a cat? Of course not, but it's difficult to know why an individual buys an item and for whom it's intended. Gifts wreak havoc with recommendation engines.

The matter of time
> It's not enough for a computer to know what you want. It must also know when you want it.

The evolution of need
> The products we need and the knowledge we seek evolves over time. Today's headline quickly becomes yesterday's news. Future use is hard to predict due to the erratic, mercurial nature of relevance decay.

The concerns of privacy
> There are limits to the amount of personal data we are willing to share in return for tailored services.

These are serious problems, and yet we should not allow the perils of personalization so defined to keep us from exploring the surrounding territories of push. For if we embrace a broader definition that encompasses social and political dimensions, personalization becomes much more interesting and important. In fact, the percentage of information we actively pull toward us is relatively small. Most of our knowledge is pushed at us by the highly personalized mix of influences that composes our surrounding environment:

People

Our family members, friends, teachers, bosses, and colleagues serve as filters of information and sources of inspiration.

Organizations

Corporate culture plays a powerful role in shaping an individual's interests and perspectives over time.

Geography

The countries, cities, and neighborhoods in which we live exert substantial influence over our politics, our knowledge, and our beliefs.

Media

From books to television to the Web, the technologies of communication that surround us change us, for better or worse.

Every day, we are exposed to stories, news, images, songs, billboards, presentations, speeches, jokes, warnings, analysis, opinion, and advice. As these messages and experiences flow through our doors of perception, they leave us with fragments of memory and insight. As the Greek philosopher Heraclitus once noted, "No man ever steps in the same river twice, for it's not the same river, and he's not the same man."

Ebb and Flow

Markets are conversations. People exchange goods, services, ideas, and values in an intricate dance of push and pull. And as technology disrupts and transforms the marketplace, only those who listen carefully will profit from this persistent disequilibrium between supply and demand. There is no substitute for the richness and intimacy of human conversation, person to person, one on one. But increasingly, our conversations are mediated by technology and co-opted by corporations. In today's world of stealth marketing and ambient advertising, we are without a doubt, unbalanced. Push is drowning out pull. Messages adorn every surface. And it's driving us bananas. Marshall McLuhan famously remarked, "the medium is the message." In today's crazy world, where bananas have become a medium, what may we ask is the message?

But we do have the ability to push back. In 1993, the United States Congress passed the Space Advertising Prohibition Act. Apparently, we decided that mile-long mylar billboards boosted into orbit and visible from planet earth crossed *the line*. And in 2003, the Federal Trade Commission began enforcing the National Do Not Call Registry. Within months, over 55 million consumers had signed up to block telemarketers from crossing *the line* into their homes. Unfortunately, we have not yet figured out how to stop spam from invading our inboxes. That is our next battle and our aim is clear. In the words of Winston Churchill, who once helped rid the British of the scourge of spam:

> It is victory, victory at all costs, victory in spite of all terror, victory, however long and hard the road may be; for without victory, there is no survival.

To win this war, we must focus on findability, for in the complex relationships between push and pull, there's real potential to improve the signal-to-noise ratio of our communications and consequently help both sender and receiver. Useful personalization, like relevant information retrieval, is difficult, but not impossible. We are making progress. We are increasingly able to control our experiences and focus our attention.

Of course, the battlefield is constantly changing. TiVo and RSS let us skip the ads, so the ads migrate into the content. Google delivers a better search but for how long? It's an ultra-competitive marketplace of fickle consumers and disruptive technologies where nobody knows what lies around the corner.

And, at the seashore between the land of atoms and the sea of bits, there rises an Internet of objects we can barely imagine. Objects precisely located in space and time. Objects that ingest their own metadata. A world of useful, usable, desirable, findable, accessible, credible objects forged by the union of engineering, marketing, and design.

In this wonderful world of everyware, we will enjoy an unprecedented ability to pull people, places, products, and ideas into our attention, but we will also face new dangers as others find creative ways to push unwanted messages and experiences into our lives. The path to ambient findability promises great adventure. Perhaps, along the way, we will learn as Lao Tzu counseled, to be still like a mountain and flow like a great river.

CHAPTER 6

The Sociosemantic Web

*Man's achievements rest upon
the use of symbols.*
—Alfred Korzybski

In 1988, sociologist Susan Leigh Star coined the term "boundary object" to describe artifacts or ideas that are shared but understood differently by multiple communities. Though each group attaches a different meaning to the boundary object, it serves as a common point of reference and a means of translation. A dead bird may be the catalyst for communication between amateur bird watchers and professional epidemiologists. A vision of sustainable development may inspire politicians, environmentalists, builders, and business leaders to engage in negotiation and collaboration. The magic of the boundary object lies in its ability to build shared understanding across social categories.

In the 1990s, the Internet emerged as a powerful boundary object, uniting early adopters in a global conversation about the future of information, communication, and commerce. Back in the text-only days of Gopher and WAIS, the Internet was a special club. Only a few belonged. Most of the world had never heard of the Internet, and many who did casually dismissed it as a playground for geeks. This rejection only strengthened the bonds of the inspired. We were amazed by the Internet. We could download software from Berkeley, send email to Moscow, and retrieve documents from Sydney. We wanted to learn everything about the Internet: where it came from, how it worked, and what it could do. We imagined the future of the Internet and its potential to change the world.

It was small club, and yet the only cost of membership was interest. In the tradition of the true believer, we wanted the club to grow. Ask a question, show sincere interest, and you're in: a bona fide member of the Internet society. It was a small club, and yet its membership expanded across all geographic, political, ethnic, sexual, religious, ideological, disciplinary, and professional lines, as Figure 6-1 suggests. We were academics, practitioners, programmers, architects, librarians, and designers. Our diversity went largely unnoticed, as we rarely met in person, but when it did surface, it was often viewed as a positive. It was cool to learn that a distinguished journalist, an elderly politician, or a young Lithuanian woman had joined the club. Every addition validated the vision.

"On the Internet, nobody knows you're a dog."

Figure 6-1. The famous Internet cartoon by Peter Steiner from the July 5, 1993 issue of The New Yorker (© The New Yorker Collection 1993 Peter Steiner from cartoonbank. com. All rights reserved.)

And then in 1993, NCSA Mosaic and its multimedia version of the World Wide Web launched cyberspace into mainstream consciousness. Those were heady days, as the first Internet stories appeared in major newspapers, magazines, and television newscasts. I still recall the contagious enthusiasm of the early Internet World conferences, during which tens of thousands gathered to learn about and celebrate this global network of networks. Milestone followed milestone: Netscape, Yahoo!, eBay, Google. It was an exciting time, but it was also the beginning of the end for the Internet society. Commercialism supplanted idealism, and the club grew so big that membership lost its privileges.

Today, the society is fragmented into myriad communities of practice, and the Internet's power to serve as boundary object is diminished. Professional specialization has led to a divergence of vision and vocabulary. Narrowly circumscribed groups develop coded languages that optimize communication between insiders at the expense of transparency for outsiders. And when these groups interact, they often talk past one another without doing the hard work necessary to translate, understand, and cooperate. This insularity can be disheartening, and yet it presents great opportunity for boundary spanners who are willing to serve as a bridge by linking ideas and people across divided networks.

Us and Them

This opportunity to connect and collaborate is particularly evident in the snarky crossfire between the Semantic Web and social software communities. On one side, we have the World Wide Web Consortium (W3C) led by Tim Berners-Lee and an international corps of software developers involved with or sympathetic to Semantic Web activity. In opposition, we have loosely joined swarms of bloggers and social software advocates, led symbolically if not spiritually by evangelists such as Clay Shirky and David Weinberger.

Though the roots of this argument run deep, this specific branch of debate began in 2001 with a *Scientific American* article called "The Semantic Web," which was authored by Tim Berners-Lee, James Hendler, and Ora Lassila.[*] In this landmark article, the authors articulated an ambitious and engaging vision for the future of the World Wide Web. And make no mistake, this article made an impact. After all, TBL isn't just some academic geek with a dream. This guy *invented* the World Wide Web. He's been knighted by Queen Elizabeth II. He's Sir Tim to the likes of us. And *Scientific American* isn't just any publication. Established in 1845, it's the oldest continuously published magazine in the United States. Former writers include Albert Einstein, Francis Crick, Jonas Salk, and Linus Pauling. The print edition boasts over 650,000 subscribers worldwide. Newsstand sales are more than *Fortune*

---

[*] "The Semantic Web" by Tim Berners-Lee, James Hendler, and Ora Lassila. *Scientific American*, May 17, 2001. Available at *http://sciam.com*.

and *Business Week* combined. And the online version receives over eight million page views a month. Let's just say this vision carried clout.

The article begins with a compelling scenario of human and computer cooperation:

> The entertainment system was belting out the Beatles' "We Can Work It Out" when the phone rang. When Pete answered, his phone turned the sound down by sending a message to all the other *local* devices that had a *volume control*. His sister, Lucy, was on the line from the doctor's office: "Mom needs to see a specialist and then has to have a series of physical therapy sessions. Biweekly or something. I'm going to have my agent set up the appointments." Pete immediately agreed to share the chauffeuring.

A medley of Semantic Web agents proceed to work with Pete, Lucy, and one another to select a physical therapist and schedule a series of appointments for Mom:

> The agent promptly retrieved information about Mom's *prescribed treatment* from the doctor's agent, looked up several lists of *providers*, and checked for the ones *in-plan* for Mom's insurance within a *20-mile radius* of her *home* and with a *rating* of *excellent* or *very good* on trusted rating services. It then began trying to find a match between available *appointment times* (supplied by the agents of individual providers through their Web sites) and Pete's and Lucy's busy schedules.

Eventually, the humans and their agents work out a plan, and the authors go on to explain how the Semantic Web will "bring structure to the meaningful content of Web pages, creating an environment where software agents roaming from page to page can readily carry out sophisticated tasks for users." To support automated reasoning, sets of inference rules must be combined with ontologies and structured knowledge representation, an artificial intelligence approach that "has not yet changed the world." They note that "to realize its full potential it must be linked into a single global system." Finally, the authors put the subject into context, explaining that "properly designed, the Semantic Web can assist the evolution of human knowledge as a whole." This was a serious *big picture* dream, and many in the software development world rallied behind its call to action.

Upon reading the article in 2001, I recall feeling a strange mix of exhilaration and skepticism. On one hand, rising from the dotcom ashes, there was this glorious vision for the future of the Web. On the other hand, as an information architect educated in library science, I harbored more than a few reservations about its ontological underpinnings. As an IA, I knew all about the false promises of AI. The Semantic Web meme was implanted in my brain, but it itched uncomfortably. And I wasn't the only troubled host.

It took a while, but in 2002, David Weinberger decided to scratch his itch with a rebuttal entitled "The Semantic Argument Web: What Really Scares Me."[*] In his brief article, David explained that TBL had been "drawn into one of the stickiest of AI morasses: knowledge representation" and offered up the following prophecy:

> I fear that the Semantic Web will go the way of SGML and for basically the same reason: normalization of metadata works real well in confined applications where the payoff is high, control is centralized, and discipline can be enforced. In other words: not the Web.

To his credit, with typical humor and humility, David noted:

> Much of the discussion of the Semantic Web is over my head and is being conducted by certified geniuses who are *much* more likely to be right than I am.

Semantic Web Disease

It starts with a scratchy throat, and (if not treated promptly) progresses to a full-blown belief that content creators everywhere will work together in harmony, and speak with one (meta-)voice. In its origins (in particular, the belief that if we understand what a name/symbol/tag means, then programs will too), it may be related to certain disorders of the AI family. The afflicted are often unaware of its progress, since when applied to small, cohesive communities of technically informed, well-meaning individuals...the beliefs actually make some sense....So do yourself a favor, and ask your doctor about the free (Semantic Web Disease) screen when you get your next mental checkup.

—Excerpt from a blog posting by Tim Converse at *http://timconverse.com/*.

The sparks really began to fly in 2003 when social software guru Clay Shirky launched a much less diplomatic attack in "The Semantic Web, Syllogism, and Worldview" in which he asked "what is the Semantic Web good for?" and promptly replied, "The Semantic Web is a machine for creating syllogisms."[†] He explained that a syllogism is a form of logic, first described by

---

[*] "The Semantic Argument Web" by David Weinberger. Available at *http://64.28.79.69/read/ swiftkick/column.html?ArticleID=421*.

[†] "The Semantic Web, Syllogism, and Worldview" by Clay Shirky. From *http://www.shirky.com/ writings/semantic_syllogism.html*.

Aristotle, whereby new conclusions can be deduced by recombining previous assertions. For example, the canonical syllogism is:

Humans are mortal

Greeks are human

Therefore, Greeks are mortal

Clay then eviscerated Aristotelian logic and deductive reasoning, illustrating the many ways they can lead down the path of syllogistic silliness, and concluded:

This is the promise of the Semantic Web—it will improve all the areas of your life where you currently use syllogisms. Which is to say, almost nowhere.

As if that wasn't bad enough, he described the Semantic Web as a shared worldview embedded in metadata and "political philosophy masquerading as code." Needless to say, this article did not endear Clay to members of the Semantic Web community. A brief but ugly period of Shirky slapping ensued, and things promised to spiral out of control, forging an even greater divide between communities.

But they didn't. Instead, some thoughtful individuals stepped into the fray and seized the opportunity to use the Semantic Web as a boundary object to build shared understanding. In particular, Paul Ford's wonderfully lucid response to Clay's article helped many (including myself) better understand the real value and potential of technologies and activities within the W3C's Semantic Web umbrella.* And Peter Van Dijck's diligent synthesis cleverly illustrated key themes and metaphors in the Semantic Web discussion.†

By moving beyond the two-value orientation of good and bad, right and wrong, us and them, these boundary spanners constructively advanced the dialog between communities. They showed that while some of the most lofty goals espoused in the *Scientific American* article are unrealistic, much of the work on triple storage, trust metrics, semantic disambiguation, and ontology exchange may prove worthwhile. And of course, many of the associated standards such as XML, XHTML, RDF, FOAF, OWL, RSS, CSS, and URIs are already in widespread use and together are shaping a more well-formed Web.

---

* "A Response to Clay Shirky's 'The Semantic Web, Syllogism, and Worldview,'" by Paul Ford. Available at *http://www.ftrain.com/ContraShirky.html*.

† "Themes and Metaphors in the Semantic Web Discussion" by Peter Van Dijck. Available at *http://www.poorbuthappy.com/ease/semantic/*.

As interface stands on the shoulders of infrastructure, tomorrow's user experience will rest on the foundation of today's Semantic Web technologies. The ability to separate descriptive, structural, and administrative metadata from content, presentation, and behavior is a tremendous boon to information architects. We have yet to fully leverage the semantic value of structural metadata in our search and navigation systems. XML has this findability potential baked right in. Which brings us to the hallowed ground of metadata that divides and unites communities. Metadata lies at the heart of the Semantic Web's ability to serve as boundary object, for it is the colorful swirl of ontologies, taxonomies, and folksonomies that brings us, cursing and cussing, to the same table.

The Social Life of Metadata

Traditionally, librarians and archivists have used the term metadata for "descriptive information used to index, arrange, file, and improve access to a library's or museum's resources."[*] This use derives from the Greek prefix *meta*, which translates as "with, among, after, or behind." In this sense, metadata accompanies but is not essential to the data itself. The classic example is the card catalog, which employs metadata to enable title, author, and subject access to a library's physical collection of materials. This use dates back to 650 B.C. in Ninevah, when king Assurbanipal constructed a palace library of over 30,000 clay tablets with a crude subject catalog and descriptive bibliography. Of course, broadly defined, metadata is as old as language itself. When we assign names to individuals, places, and possessions, we are tagging those objects with metadata. A library card catalog, shown in Figure 6-2, is a vast collection of metadata.

Metadata has many forms and purposes. Administrative metadata supports document management and workflow. Structural metadata enables single source publishing and flexible display of content. And descriptive metadata permits access and use. Put simply, we employ a word or phrase to describe the subject of a document for the purposes of retrieval. We try to concisely encapsulate its *aboutness* now to support findability later.

It is metadata's ability to help people find what they need that has driven a resurgence of interest, from the ontologies of the Semantic Web to the folksonomies of social software. Despite reaching for different solutions, these

[*] "Defining Metadata" by A.J. Gilliland-Swetland. In M. Baca (ed.), *Introduction to Metadata: Pathways to Digital Information* (1998), Getty Information Institute, Los Angeles, CA, p. 41.

Figure 6-2. A traditional library card catalog

communities face similar problems. They are using new tools to grapple with the ancient challenges of language, representation, and classification. Unfortunately, they often fail to learn from the past and from one another. These groups rarely talk to one another, and when they do, they speak in different tongues. The state of debate about structure and semantics in cyberspace is reminiscent of the ill-fated Tower of Babel, shown in Figure 6-3. Hopefully, we can use metadata as a boundary object, to foster translation, build shared understanding, and encourage real social progress.

Figure 6-3. "The Tower of Babel" by Pieter Brueghel the Elder (Kunsthistorisches Museum, Wein oder KHM, WLEN)

Taxonomies

The history of metadata is inextricably interwoven with hierarchy, for the organization of ideas and objects into categories and subcategories is fundamental to human experience. We classify to understand. Tree structures, like the one in Figure 6-4, lie at the roots of our consciousness. It is impossible to conceive of intelligence without the parent-child relationship.

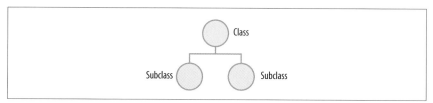

Figure 6-4. A simple taxonomy

In a formal taxonomy, a single *root node* sits atop the hierarchy. Properties flow from class to subclass through the principle of inheritance. Each object and category is assigned a single location within the taxonomy. We live at an address within a nested hierarchy of streets, cities, states, and countries. We exist as Homo sapiens within the taxa of domain, kingdom, phylum, subphylum, class, order, family, genus, and species.

Of course, the world doesn't always cooperate with this Platonic approach to classification. Fish with lungs. Mammals that lay eggs. Documents about multiple topics. Words with many meanings. Meanings with many words. Reality confounds mutually exclusive classifications, and so we find ourselves debating which existing category works best or defining new categories to allow a perfect fit. Lumpers and splitters have been haggling over the Linnaean taxonomy of living things for the past few centuries.[*]

So, aided by the flexibility of digital information systems, we have adapted our strategies to accommodate reality. We permit disciplined *polyhierarchy*, allowing a limited set of objects and classes to be cross-listed in multiple categories, as shown in Figure 6-5.

We embrace *faceted classification*, shown in Figure 6-6, using multiple fields or "facets" to describe the objects within our collections. First defined in the 1930s by Indian librarian S.R. Ranganathan, faceted classifications have

---

[*] Lumpers place roughly similar items in the same category. Splitters insist on creating new categories to accommodate distinctions. To learn more, see "Lumpers and Splitters" in the Wikipedia at *http://en.wikipedia.org/wiki/Lumpers_and_splitters.*

The Platypus Paradox

In 1799, the Department of Natural History at the British Museum received a bizarre animal specimen from Captain John Hunter in Australia. The scientific taxonomists were at first convinced that a skilled Asian taxidermist had sewn the bill of a duck to the skin of a mole as a hoax. This furry, warm-blooded creature with avian and reptilian features confounded naturalists for years. In 1836, a sighting by Charles Darwin while visiting Australia aboard the Beagle injected the platypus into the fiery debates between evolutionists and creationists. Eventually, the platypus found a taxonomic home as one of four extant monotremes, the only mammals that lay eggs rather than birthing live young. Interestingly, the semi-aquatic platypus is also one of the few mammals with a sense of electroception: it locates its prey by detecting their body electricity.

Of course, the Australian aboriginals use different names for this chimera, such as mallangong, boondaburra, and tambreet. And in the aboriginal language of Dyirbal, the platypus belongs in the Balan category along with women, bandicoots, dogs, echidna, some snakes, most birds, fireflies, scorpions, crickets, the hairy mary grub, anything connected with water or fire, and some trees.

—*Women, Fire, and Dangerous Things* by George Lakoff.
University of Chicago Press (1990), p. 93

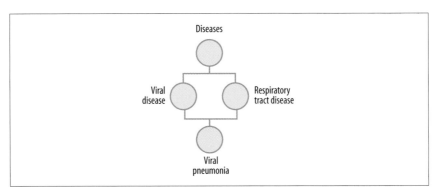

Figure 6-5. Polyhierarchy in Medline

flourished in digital domains, where objects can exist simultaneously in many locations. On the Web, we rely on this relational approach to accommodate navigation that varies by user and task. Rather than stuffing content into mutually exclusive buckets, we apply structural and semantic metadata.

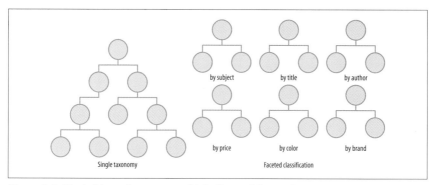

Figure 6-6. Single hierarchy versus multiple (faceted) hierarchies

And, we develop *controlled vocabularies* to manage the ambiguity of language. For our preferred terms, we define equivalence relationships to handle synonyms (variant terms that are equivalent for the purposes of retrieval) and we specify associative relationships to support *see also* links (often used for cross-sell and up-sell) that lead beyond hierarchy, creating structures like those shown in Figure 6-7.

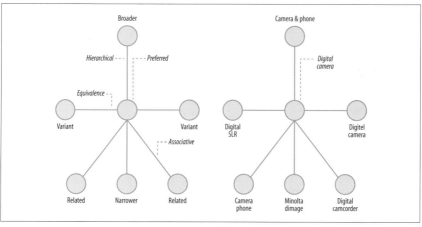

Figure 6-7. Thesaurus terms and relationships

Finally, as information architects, we recognize that by designing these structures, we are not just enabling findability. Classification systems also facilitate understanding, influence identity, and claim authority. Product taxonomies, brand architectures, and enterprise vocabularies are intimately connected to strategy and competitive advantage, as shown in Figure 6-8. And by advancing a particular worldview, all subject taxonomies are inherently political, though not all are as overt or funny as that shown in Figure 6-9.

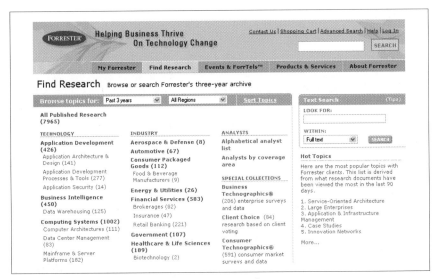

Figure 6-8. Faceted taxonomies at Forrester Research

As George Lakoff argues, "There is nothing more basic than categorization to our thought, perception, action, and speech." As we explore the potential of the Semantic Web, we should not leave these lessons of taxonomies hidden in the history of metadata.

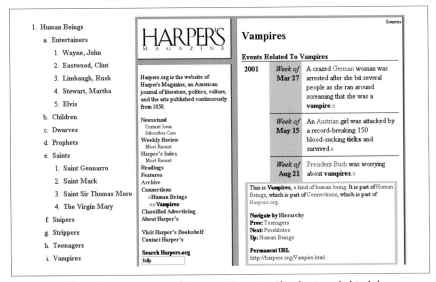

Figure 6-9. The subject taxonomy of Harpers Magazine (for the story behind the taxonomy, see "A New Website for Harper's Magazine" by Paul Ford at http://www.ftrain.com/AWebSiteForHarpers.html)

Ontologies

But, that's not to say there isn't value in a fresh approach that puts digital objects, computers, and the Internet at the center. After all, it's inevitable that controlled vocabulary standards such as Z39.19, which was first published in 1974, carry some atomic baggage into the time of bits.[*] In contrast, Semantic Web standards are born digital, developed by people with an intimate understanding of code and networks. And to their credit, these folks recognized the mission critical nature of taxonomies from the very beginning. Of course, the classic hierarchical model was overly limiting in a world of bits, so they decided to support the value-added model of ontologies:

> In philosophy, an ontology is a theory about the nature of existence, of what types of things exist....Artificial intelligence and Web researchers have co-opted the term....The most typical kind of ontology for the Web has a taxonomy and a set of inference rules.[†]

Today, the most visible applications of this model are found in Resource Description Framework (RDF), a W3C standard for describing and exchanging metadata. The structure of any expression in RDF is a collection of triples, each consisting of a subject, a predicate, and an object. They are used to make assertions that particular things have properties with certain values. These triples are specified with XML tags. Each is identified by a Universal Resource Identifier (URI) so definitions are unique and widely accessible. This triple storage model, shown in Figure 6-10, provides a powerful and flexible way of defining entities and the relationships between those entities.

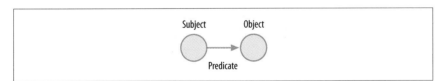

Figure 6-10. The RDF graph data model of triples

For instance, we can define a formal hierarchical relationship as follows:

Subject	Predicate	Object
Platypus	is a member of	Monotremata

---

[*] "Guidelines for the Construction, Format, and Management of Monolingual Controlled Vocabularies." Available at *http://www.niso.org/standards/resources/Z39-19.html*.

[†] Berners-Lee, *http://sciam.com*.

But we can just as easily specify equivalence and associative relationships:

Subject	Predicate	Object
Platypus	is synonymous to	Boondaburra
Platypus	is related to	Echidna

In fact, using this model, we can venture beyond the generic associative relationships of traditional thesauri. Triples permit an infinite array of typed relationships. This is an exciting quality of XML and RDF. Support for taxonomies, controlled vocabularies, faceted classifications, and rich semantic relationships is built into the infrastructure. It's an information architect's dream. Even better, findability is part of the stated goal. TBL explains that ontologies can be used "to improve the accuracy of Web searches—the search program can look for only those pages that refer to a precise concept instead of all the ones using ambiguous keywords."* And Tim Bray, coauthor of the XML specification, positions RDF encoding of metadata as "the right way to find things."†

Librarians were quick to see the value. In 1995, the Online Computer Library Center (OCLC) held a joint workshop with the National Center for Supercomputing Applications (NCSA) in Dublin, Ohio to discuss how to use semantic metadata to improve search and retrieval on the Web. These discussions eventually led to the creation of the Dublin Core Metadata Standard, which defines a simple element set for describing networked resources.‡ This metadata schema can be encoded in HTML, XML, and RDF. It fits perfectly with the triple storage model, as shown in Figure 6-11.

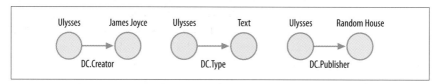

Figure 6-11. Dublin Core in RDF triples

In short, we've got a robust XML infrastructure and a metadata standard carefully crafted to be simple, extensible, and widely applicable across domains. This is an amazing foundation upon which to build applications and leverage vocabularies. So, why have the Semantic Web, RDF, and

---

* Berners-Lee, *http://sciam.com*.

† "What is RDF?" by Tim Bray. Available at *http://www.xml.com/lpt/a/2001/01/24/rdf.html*.

‡ The 16 elements include: Title, Creator, Subject, Description, Publisher, Contributor, Date, Type, Format, Identifier, Source, Language, Relation, Coverage, Rights, and Audience. To learn more, visit *http://dublincore.org/*.

Dublin Core failed to change the world? Why are they not an integral component of every web project? Why is there a sense of unmet expectations?

Some blame the complexity of RDF syntax. Some fault the lofty visions of early evangelists. Others charge the widespread misunderstanding of scope, arguing for a sole focus on machine-machine rather than human-machine or human-human interaction. There is validity to all these claims, and yet the full explanation runs wider and deeper.

First, the vast majority of information systems do not warrant the application of structured metadata and controlled vocabularies. Our primary organizing principles are epitomized by piles and files. We pile stuff on our desks and tables and floors, linear graphs in reverse chronological order. And we file stuff in cabinets and folders and directories, simple taxonomies instantiated analogously in atoms and bits. In fact, many of the world's largest corporate web sites still rely primarily on the rudimentary hierarchical model of buckets within buckets. Most of the world will never be ready for the Semantic Web. And we're still waiting for the few that constitute the rest to catch up.

Second, and closely related, the design of shared classification systems is surprisingly complex, messy, and expensive. In this sense, it is appropriate that the architects of the Semantic Web chose the term *ontology*, which in philosophy refers to the branch of metaphysics that studies the nature of reality and the basic categories of existence. What does it mean to exist? What are objects? What attributes are core? This novel vision of knowledge representation is rooted in the ancient theory of Socrates, Plato, and Aristotle. It is this legacy of deductive reasoning and syllogisms that drew Clay Shirky's fire. But as the philosopher Ludwig Wittgenstein argued, the root cause of these ontological challenges lies not only in semantics but also in the underlying logic of classification:

> Consider for example, the proceedings we call games. I mean board games, card games, ball games, Olympic games, and so on. What is common to them all?*

With this simple question, Wittgenstein exposes the fallacy of rules-based definition, and leads us toward the articulation of modern prototype theory best presented in Lakoff's *Women, Fire, and Dangerous Things*. In short, most categories we employ in everyday life are defined by fuzzy cognitive models rather than objective rules. In the vein of family resemblance, members may be related without sharing any common property. Consequently, we have membership gradience and centrality: some categories have degrees of

---

* *Philosophical Investigations* by Ludwig Wittgenstein. Macmillan (1953), p. 31.

membership, and some members are better examples than others. As Lakoff attests, the ways we categorize are rooted in language and culture. In fact, the title of his book was inspired by the Australian aboriginal language Dyirbal, which has a category, Balan, that includes women, fire, and dangerous things. It also includes birds that are not dangerous, as well as exceptional animals, such as the platypus, bandicoot, and echidna. In the vocabulary of high tech, localization requires classification as well as translation.

In addition, the design of taxonomies and ontologies is inherently political and moral. As Geoffrey Bowker and Susan Leigh Star explain in *Sorting Things Out*:

> Each standard and each category valorizes some point of view and silences another. This is not inherently a bad thing—indeed it is inescapable. But it is an ethical choice, and as such it is dangerous—not bad but dangerous.[*]

There are many ways to label and organize any collection of information. Is Taiwan a country? Is a tomato a vegetable? Where's the line between terrorist and freedom fighter? Do we really care about the subtle distinctions between Syrah, Merlot, and Pinot Noir? Aren't they all just red wines? It depends who you ask. Very few domains are exempt from this complexity of grouping and granularity. Machines may talk precisely with one another, but humans must supply the vocabulary and ultimately derive the value. At the end of the day, the Web, semantic or otherwise, is about human cooperation. Markets are conversations. Hyperlinks subvert hierarchy. The Web is alive. Or at least that's the story you'll hear from the swarms of social software buffs buzzing around the blogosphere.

Folksonomies

Since mob indexing emerged from the ether of social software, it's worth exploring this broad sociotechnical phenomenon before focusing on folksonomies. The notion of people using computers to collaborate can be traced back to 1945 and the memex of Vannevar Bush, which allowed people to share "trails" in hypertext.[†] The concept wove its way through the subsequent decades, gaining prominence in the 1980s under the banners of groupware and computer supported cooperative work. The term "social software" was first used by the nanotechnology pioneer K. Eric Drexler at the Hypertext '87 conference:

---

[*] *Sorting Things Out: Classification and its Consequences* by Geoffrey C. Bowker and Susan Leigh Star. MIT Press (2000), p.5.

[†] "Tracing the Evolution of Social Software" by Christopher Allen. Available at *http://www.lifewithalacrity.com/2004/10/tracing_the_evo.html*.

A system that enables users to automatically display some links and hide others (based on user-selected criteria) is filtered hypertext. This implies support for what may be termed social software, including voting and evaluation schemes that provide criteria for later filtering.... The possibilities for hypertext-based social software seem broad.[*]

But it wasn't until 2002 that the term came into common usage, sparked by a "Social Software Summit" organized by our friend Clay Shirky, who subsequently published his definition in a brilliant article entitled "Social Software and the Politics of Groups":

> Social software, software that supports group communications, includes everything from the simple CC: line in email to vast 3D game worlds like EverQuest, and it can be as undirected as a chat room, or as task-oriented as a wiki (a collaborative workspace). Because there are so many patterns of group interaction, social software is a much larger category than things like groupware or online communities.... One of the few commonalities in this big category is that social software is unique to the internet in a way that software for broadcast or personal communications are not.[†]

While Clay deserves credit as a catalyst, the sublime concentration of reactants made a phase transition inevitable. Blogs, comments, trackback, referrer logs, backward links, PageRank, Daypop, Slashdot, Technorati, Ryze, Friendster, LinkedIn, Wikipedia: an amazing wealth of lightweight tools for personal publishing, interaction, social feedback, conversation discovery, and reputation management had appeared seemingly overnight. Arguably, we had seen some of this before in communities like Usenet and The WELL. But at the dawn of the 21st century, the sheer scale and emergent richness of social software on the World Wide Web launched us past the proverbial tipping point. As one individual commented on David Weinberger's blog:

> The change isn't occurring in software, it's occurring in people's minds. Finally the guy who loves to make wooden ships in the bottle is realizing there's a ton of other ship builders out there and some of them live in his town.[‡]

There's tremendous excitement and activity at this intersection of social networks and information technology. Millions of bloggers swap memes in exchange for karma, whuffie, and other tokens of a reputation economy. Novel forms of discourse emerge as we experiment with Wi-Fi–enabled back-channel communications in classrooms and conferences. New toys and tools bubble to the surface with insurgent alacrity: the social bookmarks of

---

[*] Quoted in "Tracing the Evolution of Social Software" by Christopher Allen.

[†] "Social Software and the Politics of Groups" by Clay Shirky. Available at *http://www.shirky.com/writings/group_politics.html*.

[‡] Comment by Michael Pusateri (*http://cruftbox.com/*) on Joho the Blog in response to David Weinberger's post "Why Social Software Now?", which is available at *http://www.hyperorg.com/blogger/mtarchive/001451.html*.

del.icio.us, the popular photo sharing tags of Flickr. It is amidst this woof and warp of social software that folksonomies arrived. On an information architecture mailing list, Gene Smith noted the growing use of user-defined labels and tags to organize and share information, and asked "Is there a name for this kind of informal social classification?" After a brief discussion, Thomas Vander Wal replied:

> So the user-created bottom-up categorical structure development with an emergent thesaurus would become a Folksonomy?*

And so, the neologism that unites folks and taxonomy was born modestly, with a question. But upon entering the blogosphere, this word took on a life of its own, eschewing its humble origins for the glamour of David Sifry's Technorati revolution:

> Tags are a simple, yet powerful, social software innovation. Today millions of people are freely and openly assigning metadata to content and conversations. Unlike rigid taxonomy schemes that people dislike, the ease of tagging for personal organization with social incentives leads to a rich and discoverable folksonomy. Intelligence is provided by real people from the bottom-up to aid social discovery. And with the right tag search and navigation, folksonomy outperforms more structured approaches to classification.†

Even worse, this naughty ingrate of a word aligned itself with Clay Shirky in open rebellion against its parents. In a debate with Lou Rosenfeld, Shirky argued:

> The advantage of folksonomies isn't that they're better than controlled vocabularies, it's that they're better than nothing, because controlled vocabularies are not extensible to the majority of cases where tagging is needed....This is something the 'well-designed metadata' crowd has never understood…the cost of tagging large systems rigorously is crippling, so fantasies of using controlled metadata in environments like Flickr are really fantasies of users suddenly deciding to become disciples of information architecture.‡

Ouch! First he slams the Semantic Web. Then he desecrates information architecture. For a social software apostle, Clay comes across as a bit *anti-social*. Someone should tell him it's against the rules to use boundary objects as weapons.

Anyway, let's get back to this business of free tagging, mob indexing, collaborative categorization, ethnoclassification, or whatever you want to call it. The core idea is simple. Users tag objects with keywords, with the option of multiple tags, shown in Figure 6-12.

---

* Posted on the members mailing list of the Information Architecture Institute on July 24, 2004.

† "Technorati Launches Tags," a January 17, 2005 post on the blog of David Sifry, founder and CEO of Technorati, the self-described "authority on what's going on in the world of weblogs."

‡ "Folksonomies + Controlled Vocabularies" at *http://www.corante.com/many/archives/2005/01/07/folksonomies_controlled_vocabularies.php.*

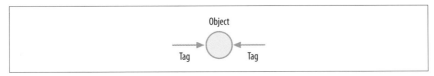

Figure 6-12. Multiple tags per object

The tags are shared and become pivots for social navigation. Users can move fluidly between objects, tags, authors, and indexers. Things get interesting when many people apply different tags to the same object and when many people apply the same tag to different objects. Let's try an example.

The information architect, Jesse James Garrett, wrote an article entitled "Ajax: A New Approach to Web Applications."* A couple of months later, 1,646 people had bookmarked this article with del.icio.us, as shown in Figure 6-13. Which, first of all, tells us it's a pretty popular article.

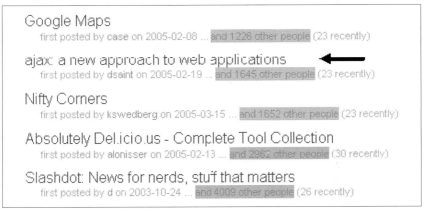

Figure 6-13. Popular links on del.icio.us

But more importantly, we can see who used which tags to describe the article. And we can follow those links to discover more about these topics and the people behind them. We can find other articles about webdev, programming, xml, ria, javascript, or flash, and even learn what other people plan to "read_later," shown in Figure 6-14. And, we can discover who else is interested in Ajax. In a sense, the object serves as a seed for emergent community.

---

* "Ajax: A New Approach to Web Applications" by Jesse James Garrett. Available at *http://www. adaptivepath.com/publications/essays/archives/000385.php.*

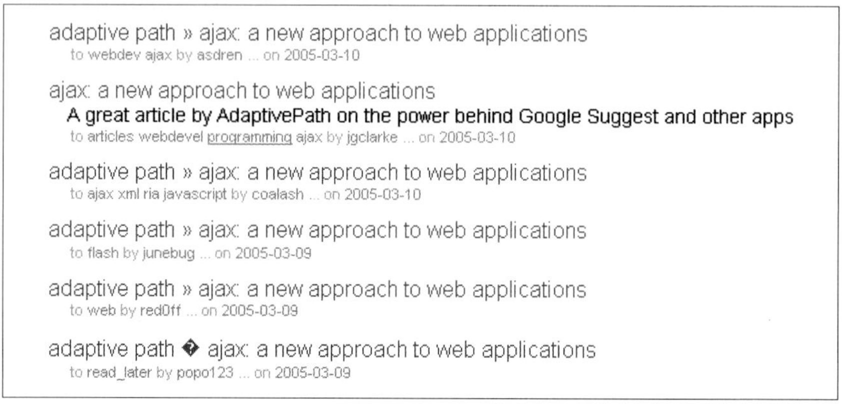

adaptive path » ajax: a new approach to web applications
to webdev ajax by asdren ... on 2005-03-10

ajax: a new approach to web applications
A great article by AdaptivePath on the power behind Google Suggest and other apps
to articles webdevel programming ajax by jgclarke ... on 2005-03-10

adaptive path » ajax: a new approach to web applications
to ajax xml ria javascript by coalash ... on 2005-03-10

adaptive path » ajax: a new approach to web applications
to flash by junebug ... on 2005-03-09

adaptive path » ajax: a new approach to web applications
to web by red0ff ... on 2005-03-09

adaptive path ◆ ajax: a new approach to web applications
to read_later by popo123 ... on 2005-03-09

Figure 6-14. Links to Jesse's article on del.icio.us

Similarly, we can view a list of other articles or objects that have been tagged with the keyword "ajax." This helps us find other people who are talking about this topic, sometimes from a very different point of view, as shown in Figure 6-15.

You got your Ajax in my Ruby
first posted by rvr on 2005-04-01 ... and 106 other people (25 recently)

Edit in Place with JavaScript and CSS
first posted by garrett on 2005-03-29 ... and 240 other people (22 recently)

XML.com: Very Dynamic Web Interfaces
first posted by amblin on 2005-02-10 ... and 1087 other people (15 recently)

Ajax From a Different Point of View
first posted by dperdue on 2005-03-22 ... and 19 other people (15 recently)

Figure 6-15. Objects tagged with keyword "ajax"

In this way, tags serve as threads that weave a disparate collection of objects together, as shown in Figure 6-16, creating an emergent category that's defined from the bottom up: a folksonomy. And, what's great is that we didn't have to pay (or wait for) librarians, ontologists, or other members of the "well-designed metadata crowd" to impose a top-down hierarchy.

Folksonomies flourish in the cornucopia of the commons without noticeable cost. They introduce a wonderful element of serendipity into web navigation, and serve as leading indicators of interest and activity. A hot tag

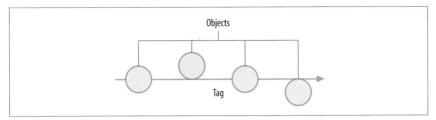

Figure 6-16. Multiple objects per tag

suggests a meme on the move, and a picture tells a thousand words. These days, it seems everybody's reading the Flickr tea leaves.[*]

Forget about ontologies and taxonomies. Folksonomies are the future. As David Weinberger puts it, "The old way creates a tree. The new rakes leaves together." And I have to agree with David. The metaphor is perfect. Because we know what happens to the beautiful piles of leaves we shuffle through each autumn. They rot. And they return to the ground, to become food for trees, which come in myriad shapes and sizes, and offer great value, and live for a very long time. Folksonomies are great for surfing what Technorati calls the World Live Web™. They are an amazing new tool for trendspotting and for revealing desire lines. And as personal bookmark tools, they're not bad for keeping found things found. But when it comes to findability, their inability to handle equivalence, hierarchy, and other semantic relationships causes them to fail miserably at any significant scale. If forced to choose between the old and new, I'll take the ancient tree of knowledge over the transient leaves of popularity (shown in Figure 6-17) any day.

But that's the beauty of the boundary object we call metadata. We don't have to choose. Ontologies, taxonomies, and folksonomies are not mutually exclusive. In many contexts, such as corporate web sites, the formal structure of ontologies and taxonomies is worth the investment. In others, like the blogosphere, the casual serendipity of folksonomies is certainly better than nothing. And in some contexts, such as intranets and knowledge networks, a hybrid metadata ecology that combines elements of each may be ideal.

This potential synergy extends beyond the genius of the AND into the concept of pace layering, perhaps best articulated by Stewart Brand. In his books *How Buildings Learn* and *The Clock of the Long Now*, Stewart explores the notion that buildings, and society as a whole, are constructs of several layers, shown in Figures 6-18 and 6-19, each with a unique and suitable rate of change.

---

[*] See Matt Jones' post at *http://blackbeltjones.typepad.com/work/2005/03/ia_summit_and_t.html*.

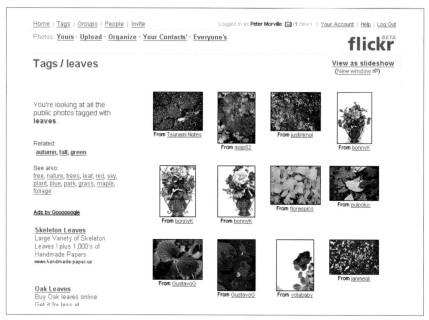

Figure 6-17. The leaves of Flickr

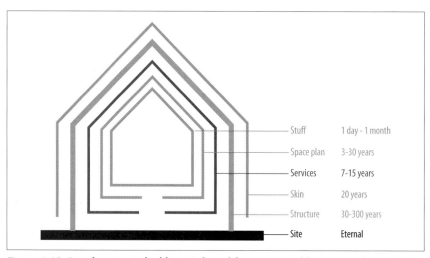

Figure 6-18. Pace layering in buildings (adapted from How Buildings Learn by Stewart Brand. Penguin Books [1995])

The slow layers provide stability. The fast layers drive innovation. The independence of speed between layers is a natural and healthy result of evolution. Imagine the alternative. How about commerce moving at the pace of government? Remember the Soviet Union?

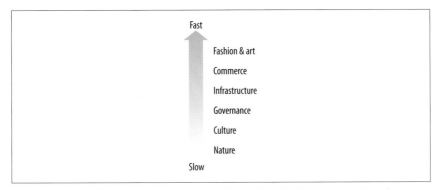

Fast

Fashion & art

Commerce

Infrastructure

Governance

Culture

Nature

Slow

Figure 6-19. Pace layering in society (adapted from The Clock of the Long Now by Stewart Brand, Basic Books [2000])

For quite some time, I have believed this concept of pace layering holds great promise within the narrower domain of web design. In this discussion of metadata, the potential for a unifying architecture is self-evident. Semantic Web tools and standards create a powerful, enduring foundation. Taxonomies and ontologies provide a solid semantic network that connects interface to infrastructure. And the fast-moving, fashionable folksonomies sit on top: flexible, adaptable, and responsive to user feedback.

And over time, the lessons learned at the top are passed down, embedded into the more enduring layers of social and semantic infrastructure. This is the future of findability and sociosemantic navigation: a rich tapestry of words and code that builds upon the strange connections between people and content and metadata.

Networks

A network is composed of nodes connected by links: islands linked by bridges, markets by trade routes, computers by phone lines, nerve cells by axons, and people by relationships. Figure 6-20 shows a very simple network. Networks play a powerful role in our lives. They influence where we go and who and what we find. This is the invisible thread that connects semantic and social networks, and has us seeking findability insights in the wilds of social network analysis.

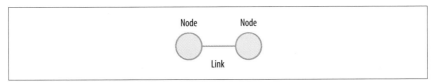

Node   Node

Link

Figure 6-20. A simple graph or network

The study of interaction between people often reveals patterns that are interesting from a findability perspective. For instance, in the example shown in Figure 6-21, we can measure:

Activity
> Susan is a "connector" with six direct links to other nodes. She is at the center of a densely connected cluster or community of practice.

Betweenness
> Claudia has only three connections but holds a powerful position as the sole "boundary spanner" between different groups.

Closeness
> Sarah and Steven have the shortest paths to all others. They have an excellent view of what's going on.

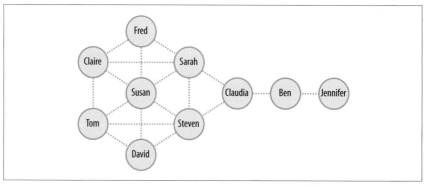

Figure 6-21. Kite network diagram (from "Social Network Analysis" by Peter Morville; available at http://semanticstudios.com/publications/semantics/000006.php)

These metrics can be applied at the level of individuals, organizations, and industries. They can also be applied to computer networks to optimize topology and to information systems to improve findability. For the "boundary spanner" in this example could just as easily be a document found in a library or through a Google search. Nodes can be people or content, and can serve as end or path, data or metadata. Articles, books, and blogs are not simply destinations, for they often serve as inverse queries that draw users to authors. We write, not just to communicate, but to enhance our own personal findability.

Another interesting pattern in social networks is the "small world" phenomenon that's been popularized by the phrase "six degrees of separation." And, in this sense, the Web is also a small world. A research study conducted in 1998 that estimated a publicly indexable Web of 800 million nodes, suggested that "any document is on average only nineteen clicks away from any other."* However, as Albert-Laszlo Barabasi explains:

> The six/nineteen degrees phrase is deeply misleading because it suggests that things are easy to find in a small world. This could not be further from the truth! Not only is the desired person or document six/nineteen links away, but so are all people or documents.[†]

According to Barabasi's calculations, if it took only a second to check a document, it would take over 300 million years to find all documents that are 19 clicks away. Small worlds don't resolve findability. We can gain more insight by understanding power laws. Remember Zipf Distributions? In self-organizing networks like human society and the Internet, many small events coexist with a few large events. On the Web, a few major hubs enjoy huge quantities of inbound links, while most web sites are barely visible in the eyes of popularity-sensing algorithms like PageRank. Of course, it's not just sites that suffer in the Siberia of the Long Tail. This is where many of the searches reside as well. Linking supply and demand in the Long Tail is a great challenge and opportunity. As Chris Anderson notes, the typical Barnes & Noble carries 100,000 titles. Yet a quarter to a third of Amazon's book sales come from *outside* its top 100,000 titles.[‡] If that's not a wake up call for marketing professionals, I'm not sure what is. Amazon, eBay, Netflix, and Google all profit by mining a million niches at the tip of this Long Tail.

But their success provides little consolation to the owners and authors of invisible nodes in the network. Consider, for instance, the Italian entrepreneur who asked me for help. He had paid a design firm to build a web site for his company. Several months later, he discovered that his site was unfindable. Even a query on the exact name of his company failed to return his site in Google. At first glance, the site was attractive enough, but a quick look under the hood revealed the problem. The text had been rendered as images in a quest for typographical control: desirability at the expense of findability.

In this simple example lies an important lesson. On the Web, the journey often begins with the destination. The user's keyword entered into a search engine must connect with a keyword in your web site, or the visit is over before it has begun. For this reason, it's worth looking more closely at the node at the end of the road we call the document.

---

* *Linked: The New Science of Networks* by Albert-Laszlo Barabasi. Perseus (2002), p. 34.

† Barabasi, p. 37.

‡ "The Long Tail" by Chris Anderson. See *http://longtail.typepad.com/the_long_tail/2005/08/a_methodology_f.html*.

Documents

Articles, books, contracts: what is common to them all? How about a song, a weather forecast, a satellite image? Where is the border between data and documents? In the digital era, at the edges of this family of artifacts, Wittgenstein's wisdom becomes clear. Basic definitions focus on written or printed information that is fixed in form. More sophisticated approaches invoke the centrality of intentionality, embracing a wider circle of less tangible, more mutable expressions of human thought. But all attempts fall short. Like most objects of consequence, the document resists definition; and in this free state, unbound by simple rules, plays an amazing role in our lives.

Historically, documents have served as power objects. Receipts and passports prove ownership and identification. Written contracts, charters, certificates, commandments, and constitutions glow with embedded authority. Their legal, moral, and symbolic value sustains our institutions of government, education, and commerce. Modern civilization is unimaginable without these instruments of communication, collaboration, and control.

Yet, many have characterized our time as the beginning of the end of documents. Deborah Juhnke, a computer forensics expert, says our "reliance on the document paradigm must change" because from a legal, evidentiary perspective, "the document is dead."[*] And information architect Gene Smith argues "the page is dying as the predominant metaphor for organizing and presenting online information."[†] From word processors to wikis, computers render documents editable and plausibly deniable. But do content management systems and rich Internet applications make them obsolete? Do documents have a future in a multi-channel world of blog posts, RSS feeds, and reusable XML chunks? Or will increased granularity, reduced latency, and transparent transitions turn pages into anachronisms? These questions gain currency in an era of mobile devices, and yet rumors of the death of the document are greatly exaggerated. Pages, documents, and the familiar document types we call "genres" will not disappear overnight. On the contrary, as John Seely Brown and Paul Duguid suggest:

> The document metaphor and documents themselves may be as important to the 'information galaxy' of cyberspace as they have been in its Gutenberg equivalent.[‡]

---

[*] "Electronic Discovery in 2010" by Deborah Juhnke. Available at *http://www.findarticles.com/p/articles/mi_qa3937/is_200311/ai_n9328751*.

[†] "Beyond the Page" by Gene Smith. Available at *http://atomiq.org/archives/2004/10/beyond_the_page.html*.

[‡] "The Social Life of Documents" by John Seely Brown and Paul Duguid. Available at *http://www.firstmonday.dk/issues/issue1/documents/*.

In fact, the document will endure as long as we do, for it is not tied to technology, but like space, time, and hierarchy, is a construct of the human mind. We understand documents. Their familiar design confers ease of use, and their integrated content and structure supports navigation. Documents are the preeminent findable objects. And whether in print or digital form, their success derives largely from their shape.

The Shape of Information

Most declarations of documental demise belie the way we actually unite form, content, and purpose to forge a genre. Technology and medium surely play a role. The affordances of clay, stone, animal skin, plant fiber, and silicon vary widely. And yet, as researchers Kevin Crowston and Marie Williams explain:

> Genre is not identical to the medium of the communication—a memo may be realized on paper or in an electronic mail message, while electronic mail may be used to deliver memos or inquiries.[*]

Consider the genres that have emerged in the print medium: maps, menus, newspapers, magazines, paperbacks, tri-fold brochures, white papers, and little black books. In theory, all could be printed on standard 8.5×11 sheets. We didn't derive these genres from the inherent properties of paper. We designed them for a purpose. Genre responds to use. The unique shape of a receipt helps a user predict value and meaning. What makes us think that XML will suddenly transform information into an amorphous gray goo that flows indiscriminately between containers and channels? We should not be seduced by the siren song of radical reusability whispered in our ears by software vendors. The ability to assemble virtual documents from digital assets on the fly does not render real documents obsolete. Single source publishing works wonders with highly structured content, and simple images, headlines, and legal notices are well-suited to reusability. But most content requires context and structure, and most authors write documents, not chunks.

In fact, new genres have already started to appear on the Web, as shown in Figure 6-22: web sites, home pages, sitemaps, FAQs, and blogs are leading indicators of genre shift. And, of course, we've imported and remixed established genres as well. Dictionaries, encyclopedias, and email memos with formal PDF reports attached have all become elements within our evolving

---

[*] "Reproduced and Emergent Genres of Communication on the World Wide Web" by Kevin Crowston and Marie Williams. Available at *http://crowston.syr.edu/papers/genres-journal.html*.

genre system in which context can be as meaningful as content. As David Levy notes:

> No document, no genre, is an island....To be a receipt is to be connected to cash registers, sellers, buyers, products, expense reports, the IRS, and so on.[*]

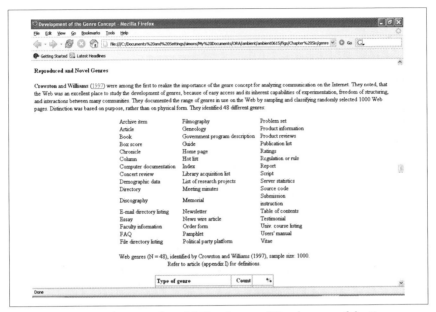

Figure 6-22. Forty-eight genres from 1,000 web pages ("Development of the Genre Concept" by Leen Breure; available at http://www.cs.uu.nl/people/leen/GenreDev/ GenreDevelopment.htm)

In this sense, digital genre plays a significant role in search and navigation. First, genre supports document findability. Filter by content type, for instance, enables users to limit their search space to press releases, product briefs, or technical reports. Second, genre supports document recognition. Upon viewing a PDF newsletter, users instantly recognize its nature and purpose. Through rapid visual identification, we know when we've found what we need. Third, genre supports navigation within a document. The familiar shape of a scientific document, shown in Figure 6-23, permits rapid scanning. We can review the abstract and then skip right to the results. Interestingly, research has shown that semantics and structure are

---

[*] *Scrolling Forward* by David Levy. Arcade (2003), p. 29.

codependent.* Structure contributes to understanding and comprehension, while meaning helps establish a sense of location. Users can tell where they are in a document from the semantic content of individual paragraphs.

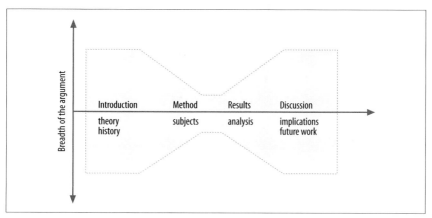

Figure 6-23. The shape of a scientific document (image from http://www.ischool.utexas. edu/~adillon/publications/journey.html)

For all these reasons, genre hasn't expired after a decade of web design, and it won't die at the hands of handhelds either. But mobile devices will catalyze further genre shift, as we develop novel forms to fit tiny screens that wander. As Peter Merholz explains "you can't just take any web page, and expect it to work within any device."† New genres will emerge at the intersection of device affordance and situational relevance. Some will stay on the desktop while others will make sense on the move. Documents and genres aren't going to disappear. In fact, they're about to become more visible.

Antelopes as Boundary Objects

The next few years will force us to revisit our conception of the document. For even as we struggle to make sense of digital genre, ubicomp will inject growing numbers of physical objects into the category of document. This notion of object as document is nothing new.‡ In 1934, Paul Otlet, a pioneer

---

* "It's the journey and the destination: shape and the emergent property of genre in evaluating digital documents" by Andrew Dillon and Misha Vaughan. Available at *http://www.ischool.utexas. edu/~adillon/publications/journey.html.*

† "Genres Hamper Mobile Internet" by Peter Merholz. Available at *http://www.peterme.com/ archives/000472.html.*

‡ "What is a Document?" by Michael Buckland. Available at *http://www.sims.berkeley.edu/ ~buckland/whatdoc.html.*

in the field of information science (then called "documentation"), extended the definition as follows:

> Graphic and written records are representations of ideas or of objects, but the objects themselves can be regarded as documents if you are informed by observation of them.*

The librarian and documentalist, Suzanne Briet, addressed this extension of meaning in a 1951 manifesto in which she asserts a document is "…evidence in support of a fact…any physical or symbolic sign, preserved or recorded, intended to represent…or to demonstrate a physical or conceptual phenomenon."† Suzanne argues that an antelope running wild on the plains of Africa is not a document. But if captured, placed in a zoo, and made an object of study, that same antelope has been transformed into a document (see Table 6-1).

Table 6-1. Suzanne Briet's analysis of objects as documents[a]

Object	Document?
Star in sky	No
Photo of star	Yes
Stone in river	No
Stone in museum	Yes
Animal in wild	No
Animal in zoo	Yes

[a] Adapted from "What is a Document?" by Michael Buckland.

As Michael Buckland explains, Briet's rules for defining when an object becomes a document are not entirely clear, but we can infer several criteria from her discussion:

Intention
Intended to be treated as evidence

Process
Processed or made into a document

Perception
Perceived as a document

Indexing
Organized within a collection of evidence

---

* *Traité de documentation* by Paul Otlet. Brussels: Editiones Mundaneum (1934), p. 217.

† *Qu'est-ce que la documentation* by Suzanne Briet. Paris: EDIT (1951).

Both Otlet and Briet were trying to include the natural objects and artifacts of zoos, museums, and libraries, without admitting the entire world into the category of document. It's interesting to review their classifications through the lens of today's technology. Let's consider Briet's antelope, for instance. What if we leave the antelope in the wild, but embed an RFID tag or attach a GPS transponder or assign it a URL? What if our antelope is indexed by Google? What if we can view it via a network of video cameras?

This is not simply an exercise in semantics, for whether we use the word "document" or not, we have already begun adding documental qualities to people, places, and objects. As Bruce Sterling notes, in reference to the "smart object" known as Rafael Macedo de la Concha, Mexico's attorney general who had RFID tags implanted in his arm (and the arms of his staff) in a bid to fight corruption through better tracking and authentication:

> It's his brain that makes him smart. It's the chip that makes him an object: cataloged, searchable, and locatable in space and time.*

We're creating a whole new taxonomy of findable objects, and our under-standing of the boundary objects we call documents will serve us well in these uncharted territories.

The End of Data

Despite this revolution at the document core, we should not focus solely on the center, for as one might expect of a boundary object, there's serious action at the edges. We're talking about the blurring at the borders between data and metadata, a phenomenon with great relevance to findability. As usual, Mr. Weinberger is on top of this trend. He writes:

> There used to be a difference between data and metadata. Data was the suit-case and metadata was the name tag on it....Data was the contents of the book and metadata was the Dewey Decimal number on its spine....[Now], all data is metadata....Data is all surface and no insides. It's all handles and no suitcase. It's a folder whose content is just another label. It's all sticker and no bumper.†

Amazon.com serves as the archetype for this intertwingling. A book listed on Amazon is far more than the words between its covers. Each record is saturated with a rich blend of semantic and social metadata designed to help you find the book you need. Formal bibliographic notations and subject classifications coexist with popularity, reputation, co-citation analysis,

---

* "Dumbing Down Smart Objects" by Bruce Sterling. *Wired Magazine*, October 2004. Available at *http://www.wired.com/wired/archive/12.10/view.html?pg=4*.

† "The End of Data?" by David Weinberger. Available at *http://www.hyperorg.com/backissues/joho-oct15-04.html#data*.

collaborative filtering, and customer reviews. And with Search Inside the Book™, Amazon has turned the page into metadata. Every word is a keyword. Each text is linked to others by a common turn of phrase. Every book enjoys membership in an infinite number of categories in this n-dimensional bookstore that boggles the mind.

But Amazon's novel use of data and metadata for navigation and competitive advantage is only the tip of the iceberg. Bruce Sterling hints at the future in his vision of the location-aware, history-enriched, auto-Googling objects he calls spimes.* This idea of history-enriched digital objects draws from the physical world, where dog-eared books, padded doorframes, and worn stairs make interaction history visible.

Wear is an emergent property of physical objects that has barely been tapped online. In fact, the markers of previous use have been largely ignored in information science. There is an exception in the rich tradition of "provenance" in archives and record management that emphasizes context over content—archivists seek to identify the office of origin and the chain of custody, and strive to preserve the "sanctity of original order"—maintaining documents as they were originally arranged.† But these archival arrangements have been applied towards evidential value and scholarly understanding, not findability.

For now, the Web is the preeminent sandbox for exploring how interaction history can support social navigation. Popularity and reputation are the most common metrics, and an assortment of high-profile examples illuminate the possibilities:

- Google uses the quality and quantity of inbound links as part of a multi-algorithmic solution to derive popularity, reputation, and ultimately relevance.
- Technorati lists the Top 100 "most authoritative" blogs ranked by the number of sources that link to each blog.
- Newsmap, shown in Figure 6-24, presents a visual representation of Google News that blends hand-picked sources with popularity algorithms to determine "relevance."
- The *New York Times* presents a ranked list of the most emailed articles.

---

* "When Blobjects Rule the Earth" by Bruce Sterling. SIGGRAPH, Los Angeles, August 2004. Available at *http://www.boingboing.net/images/blobjects.htm*.

† "The Principle of Provenance and Modern Archival Systems" by Megan Winget. Available at *http://www.unc.edu/~winget/research/provenance.pdf*.

- Wikipedia allows us to view a list of the most edited articles, thereby showcasing the more controversial people and topics of our time.
- CNET's Download.com lists the most frequently downloaded software.
- Amazon converts popular paths in the clickstream into "customers who viewed this item also viewed these items."
- Epinions lets users rate products and rate the raters, a system that enables repeat visitors to construct a personal "web of trust."
- eBay's auction system relies on reputations for ranking buyer and seller honesty.
- Slashdot's metamoderation and "karma" metric define whose articles get read.
- Flickr showcases the all time most popular tags, as well as the hot tags in the last 24 hours and over the last week.

And, many home pages list the "most popular" or "most visited" pages for their web sites. What's amazing is how effectively all of this popularity and reputation metadata contributes to widely acceptable definitions of relevance.

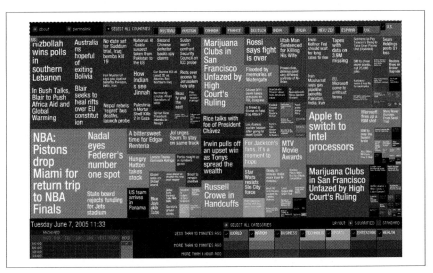

Figure 6-24. Newsmap

With respect to findability, we're comfortable trusting the wisdom of crowds. And this popularity metadata not only influences which data we find but our respect for that data as well. As studies have shown, "the findability of information biases its perceived quality."* Herein lies the dark side to this tyranny of popularity. The rich get richer, or as Barabasi puts it:

> In real networks linking is never random. Instead, popularity is attractive. Webpages with more links are more likely to be linked to again....Network evolution is governed by the subtle yet unforgiving law of preferential attachment.†

Of course, the sphere of contextual metadata extends well beyond popularity. Information about who created or edited a document, and what changes were made when by whom, can add value to the document itself. Increasingly, this bundle of data and metadata is an entity in its own right, with practical and legal substance. And, as we venture beyond the Web, spatial and temporal metadata will gain resonance. Some foundational work exists in the domain of personal information management. In the 1980s, Thomas Malone's office organization research showed the method behind the madness of our piles and files, and in particular the role of spatial location in finding and reminding.‡ And more recently, researchers at Stanford and Microsoft have explored the application of timelines, temporal landmarks, and spatial memory for document management and retrieval.§ But, at the crossroads of spatial and semantic wayfinding, we've barely scratched the surface. In an age of location-awareness, when metadata can be attached to people, possessions, and places, the findability and value of our documents and objects will be shaped by strange new forms of sociosemantic *aboutness*.

We see this already in the phenomenon of Googlebombing.** A search on "miserable failure" returns George W. Bush's presidential biography as the top hit, as demonstrated in Figure 6-25. Now, I can assure you, neither keyword appears within the biography itself. With respect to aboutness, the social campaign of linking overwhelms the semantic content of the page.

This reflects a fundamental shift in power from author to reader and from authority to popularity that is only just beginning to make waves outside the blogosphere. It will be interesting to follow the fast-developing story of this quiet, global revolution.

---

* "Manifesto for the Reputation Society" by Hassan Masum and Yi-Cheng Zhang in *First Monday* (2004). Available at *http://www.firstmonday.org/issues/issue9_7/masum/*.

† Barabasi, p. 86.

‡ "How Do People Organize Their Desks? Implications for the Design of Office Information Systems" by Thomas W. Malone (1983). *ACM Transactions on Office Information Systems*.

§ "Milestones in Time: The Value of Landmarks in Retrieving Information from Personal Stores." Available at *http://research.microsoft.com/~sdumais/SISLandmarks-Interact2003-final.pdf*. Also, "Data Mountain: Using Spatial Memory for Document Management." Available at *http://www.microsoft.com/usability/UEPostings/p153-robertson.pdf*.

** Googlebombing is an attempt to influence search result rankings on Google through a concerted campaign of linking a keyword or phrase to a particular target URL. To learn more, see *http://en.wikipedia.org/wiki/Googlebomb*.

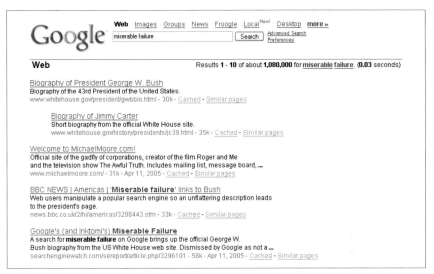

Figure 6-25. A famous example of Googlebombing

A Walk in the Park

As we build our Internet of objects, the permutations of sociosemantic metadata will create new avenues of findability. Where has this object been? Which objects were in close proximity to this object? Who touched my object? Where are they now? The era of ambient findability will overflow with metadata, as every object and location sprouts tags: social and semantic, embedded and unembedded, controlled and uncontrollable.

Imagine the sensory overload of a walk in the park. Every path shimmers with the flow of humanity. Every person drips with the scent of information: experience, opinion, karma, contacts. Every tree has a story: taxonomies and ontologies form bright lattices of logic. Desire lines flicker with unthinkable complexity in this consensual hallucination of space and nonspace, a delicious yet overwhelming sociosemantic experience.

How will we make sense of this tower of babble? In the midst of this cacophony, to whom will we listen? Who will we trust? Will we rely on formal hierarchy or free tagging, library or marketplace, cathedral or bazaar? Will we place our confidence in words or people? And are we talking about cyberspace or ubicomp? The answer lies in the question, for we will not be bound by the false dichotomy of Aristotelian logic. To manage complexity, we must embrace faceted classification, polyhierarchy, pluralistic aboutness, and pace layering. And to succeed, we must collaborate across categories, using boundary objects to negotiate, translate, and forge shared understanding.

Of course, even with all this sociosemantic cooperation, the road ahead is long and winding, with many paths not taken. Our ability to make informed decisions will depend on how we allocate attention and trust, how we define authority, and how we employ metaphor. As Alfred Korzybski, the polymathic founder of general semantics, taught us "man's achievements rest upon the use of symbols" and yet "the map is not the territory." We would do well to recall his words and meaning as we take our walk in the park.

CHAPTER 7

Inspired Decisions

No one realized that the book and the
labyrinth were one and the same.

—Jorges Luis Borges
"The Garden of Forking Paths"

I remember the summer of 1989. I was 19 years old, a sophomore biology major at Tufts University, and a transient in the home of my parents. My passions were, in no particular order, soccer, girls, literature, beer, and artificial intelligence. My summer began in the environmental lab of the Millstone nuclear power plant, where I measured the impact of thermal discharge on marine biodiversity. By day, I studied sand under a microscope, and by night, the works of Dostoevsky, Turing, Hofstadter, and Dennett.

That August, we took a family vacation to France and England. I left the sand behind, but the self-reflections of *The Mind's I* and the eternal golden braids of *Gödel, Escher, Bach* traveled with us. In fact, one of my fondest memories is of wandering with my brother through strange loops and tangled hierarchies, surrounded by the rolling green hills of the English countryside. Thinking machines, disembodied minds, silicon souls, selfish memes: we were intoxicated by metaphorical fugues, and a few pints from the local pub.

It was during these forays into artificial intelligence (AI) that I first stumbled into decision trees. A decision tree, like that shown in Figure 7-1, is a graph of choices and possible consequences. In theory, by identifying options and outcomes, and multiplying the probability and value (minus cost) of each outcome, we can reduce decisions to quantitative analysis. Of course, their utility isn't limited to humans but holds great promise for AI. After all, rational choice has long been held as a sign of intelligence. So naturally, the roots of AI, and the big wins in expert systems and game algorithms, are flush with decision trees. In fact, it was Deep Blue's ability to evaluate "leaf positions" at a rate of 200 million moves per second that enabled victory over Gary Kasparov in 1997. Before that match, the chess champion said "I'm playing for the honor of the human race." Afterward, Deep Blue remained silent.

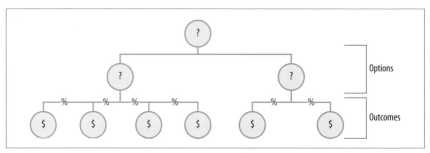

Figure 7-1. A simple decision tree

In the last half century, the prospect of thinking machines inspired significant research and novel insight into the constitution of real intelligence. So it's both natural and ironic that Herbert Simon, a founding father of the field of AI, struck the mortal blow to the classic model of rational choice and the broad applicability of decision trees. In his 1956 landmark paper, this Nobel Laureate and A.M. Turing Award recipient employed a simple organism's search for food as a metaphor for decision-making:

> It is convenient to describe the organism's life space not as a continuous surface, but as a branching system of paths, like a maze, each branch point representing a choice point. We call the selection of a branch and locomotion to the next branch point a "move."[*]

He argued that within a framework of fuzzy goals, imperfect information, and limited time, our partly rational minds adapt well enough to "satisfice" but don't generally optimize. Simon's radical theory of "bounded rationality" led not only to the demise of "homo economicus," but also to appreciation for the intricacies of human intelligence, because the simple rules of chess don't apply to the complex decisions of real life.

Simon's work anticipated the difficulties of AI, though he never gave up the dream. In an interview not long before his death in 2001, he was asked whether a computer might someday deserve a Nobel. In response, Simon said: "I see no deep reason why not."

---

[*] "Rational Choice and the Structure of the Environment" by Herbert A. Simon (1956). *Psychological Review*, vol. 63, no. 2.

Bounded Irrationality

But let's forget AI, for a time, and delve instead into the depths of human irrationality, beginning with some well-documented decision-making traps.*

Anchoring

> When considering a decision, our minds are unduly influenced by the first information we find. Initial impressions and data anchor subsequent judgments.

Confirmation

> Through selective search and perception, we subconsciously seek data that supports our existing point of view, and avoid contradictory evidence.

Memorability

> We are overly influenced by recent or dramatic events. Repetition from one or multiple sources can also influence belief, memory, and judgment.

Status quo

> Decision makers exhibit a strong bias toward conservatism, inertia, and alternatives that perpetuate the status quo. We look for reasons to do nothing.

Sunk cost

> Unwilling, consciously or not, to admit past mistakes, we make decisions in a way that justifies past choices.

We ask the wrong questions and trust the wrong sources. We substitute optimism for data. And we are influenced by peer pressure and groupthink. Decisions shape our lives, and yet they're often made in the dark, beneath the comforting veneer of rationality.

In *Blink*, Malcolm Gladwell puts a positive spin on what he calls "thin slicing" or "the ability of our unconscious to find patterns in situations and behavior based on very narrow slices of experience."[†] He contends that "if we are to improve the quality of the decisions we make, we need to accept the mysterious nature of our snap judgments."[‡] I disagree. Thin slicing is not infallible. It can have disastrous, regrettable results. And, it need not remain mysterious. We can learn more about how and why our brains work

---

* "The Hidden Traps in Decision Making" by John S. Hammond, Ralph L. Keeney, and Howard Raiffa. *Harvard Business Review*, September/October 1998.

† *Blink: The Power of Thinking Without Thinking* by Malcolm Gladwell. Little, Brown (2005), p. 23.

‡ Gladwell, p.52.

the way they do, and we can use that information to modify our behavior accordingly.

In *Harvard Business Review*, Alden Hayashi describes the role of instinct and intuition in executive decision-making, and investigates their biological basis:

> First, your mind continuously processes information that you are not consciously aware of, not only when you're asleep and dreaming but also when you're awake. This helps explain the "aha" sensation you experience when you learn something that you actually already knew....Second, your brain is intricately linked to other parts of your body through an extensive nervous system as well as through chemical signals...what we call the "mind" is really this intertwined system of brain and body. This, then, helps explain why intuitive feelings are frequently accompanied by physical reactions.[*]

Suddenly, we find ourselves back at the crossroads of evolutionary psychology and neuroscience, with brains designed by natural selection to solve ancient problems. As Leda Cosmides and John Tooby explain, "form follows function: the properties of an evolved mechanism reflect the structure of the task it evolved to solve."[†] While our rational neocortex can refocus attention from snakes to semantics, our passionate amygdala is trapped in the mind-body of the hunter-gatherer. And, it's often our most vital decisions about family, career, and health that are most influenced by emotion.

In the face of such "bounded irrationality," it's tempting to seek solace in the wisdom of crowds and the knowledge that "even if most of the people within a group are not especially well-informed or rational, it can still reach a collectively wise decision."[‡] This emergent, self-organizing network effect yields the predictive power of stock markets, and there's an irresistible elegance to the idea of collective intelligence:

> Natural selection's invisible hand created the structure of the human mind, and the interaction of these minds is what generates the invisible hand of economics.[§]

But, like thin slices, invisible hands can harm as well as help. Markets crash. Elections fail. Wars erupt. Google doesn't always deliver the best results. We should proceed cautiously before placing our lives in the invisible hands of smart mobs. The wisdom of crowds does not negate the value of bright individuals and informed decisions. On the contrary, in today's society,

---

[*] "When to Trust Your Gut" by Alden M Hayashi. *Harvard Business Review*, February 2001.

[†] "Better than Rational: Evolutionary Psychology and the Invisible Hand" by Leda Cosmides and John Tooby. *The American Economic Review*, vol. 84, no. 2.

[‡] *The Wisdom of Crowds* by James Surowiecki. Doubleday (2004), p. xiii.

[§] Cosmides and Tooby, p. 328.

information seeking and insight through pattern recognition are closely linked with intelligence, innovation, and success. In particular, the Internet offers the ability to make wise decisions through access to myriad data types and sources.

Informed Decisions

Let's say, for instance, Carol and Charles need a larger vehicle that can handle their growing family. Twin daughters are due in a couple of months. She's thinking minivan, but he suggests a Ford Explorer: the same family functionality with a much cooler look. Besides, their neighbor loves her 2004 Sport Trac, and she has three kids. Carol's almost convinced, but that evening, on impulse, she fires up her browser and starts Googling.

An hour later, Carol is making the following case to her husband:

- SUVs have a much greater risk of rolling over in an accident than passenger cars and minivans, due to their higher center of gravity. In fact, the Ford Explorer Sport Trac is among the worst, with a 34% chance of rollover in a single vehicle crash.[*]

- While rollovers affect only 3% of crashes, they account for 31% of fatalities.[†]

- Motor vehicle crashes are the leading cause of death in the United States for people aged 1 to 34; higher than fires, drownings, falls, and poisonings combined.[‡]

- The Toyota Sienna minivan, followed closely by the Honda Odyssey, is the top-rated safety pick by both the National Highway Traffic Safety Administration (NHTSA) and the Insurance Institute for Highway Safety (IIHS).[§]

Carol notes that lower insurance rates, fuel consumption, and emissions make the minivans better on both the pocketbook and the environment. And that's not all. Carol is also armed with a slew of comparative data about the Sienna and Odyssey: expert and customer reviews, popularity rankings, standard and optional equipment specifications, photos, videos, and pricing details. She's even requested a quote for a Sienna. Carol explains that this decision is really all about safety, and ultimately, Charles agrees.

---

[*] National Highway Traffic Safety Administration (NHTSA), *http://www.nhtsa.dot.gov/*.

[†] Advocates for Highway and Auto Safety, *http://www.saferoads.org*.

[‡] CDC National Center for Health Statistics, *http://www.cdc.gov/nchs/*.

[§] Autobytel, *http://www.autobytel.com/*.

This may turn out to be one of the most important decisions of their lives. And it was influenced by the availability and power of the Internet. If faced with the prospect of a trip to the local library, Carol may have gone with her husband's original suggestion. After all, we know accessibility is "the single most important variable governing the use of information."* In the spirit of our tribal ancestors, we absorb most of our information passively and rely on who we know for much of what we know. Search can be an integral part of the decision-making process. What we find influences what we do. But the first step is deciding to search, and the smallest of barriers will deter us. The primacy of accessibility is among the firmest ties that bind our rationality. We trust the informal gossip of the grapevine without seeking the analysis of experts. And our source bias feeds our anchoring, memorability, and confirmation bias to further tangle our judgment.

For all these reasons, the Internet offers us the power to make better decisions. We can quickly and easily step outside the circle of family, friends, and co-workers, in search of independent wisdom and collective intelligence. The diversity of sources, the volume of data, and the ease of access are unprecedented. We have the world at our fingertips. Of course, the Internet is not without its own prejudice. A great deal of scholarly, published, and printed content is not yet accessible. This has real impact, even in the relatively rigorous realm of scientific publishing, where online articles are cited 4.5 times more often than offline articles.† The Internet favors information that's free and digital. And, search engines introduce their own unique and often invisible dispositions. Google, for instance, employs a trade-secret, multi-algorithmic solution that favors linguistic precision and link popularity, relying on exact matches of keywords in content and links rather than subject-oriented metadata or conceptual pattern matching. And, of course, Google's answers are intertwingled with the business of advertising in a delicate and sometimes uncomfortable dance between push and pull.

Network Culture

The Internet has shifted the landscape of informed decisions, but the impact is not entirely positive. For insight into the dark side, ask librarians. They'll tell you about students who never visit the library, but instead surf the web for a few good hits, with little appreciation for the authority, accuracy,

---

* "Information Needs for Management Decision-Making." *Records Management Quarterly*. October 1993, p.15.

† "Online or Invisible?" by Steve Lawrence (2001). *Nature*, vol. 411, no. 6837, p. 521.

---

currency, and quality of their sources. They'll lament the public's lack of appetite for Boolean search. They'll complain that scholarly networked databases and peer-reviewed journals sit untouched, while Google churns out fast food for the minds of the masses. Librarians are on the front lines of an invisible struggle over our information diet and, for better or worse, the scales are not tipping in their direction. In fact, according to Peter Lyman, a distinguished professor at UC Berkeley's School of Information Management and Systems, it's already too late:

> There's been a culture war between librarians and computer scientists.
>
> And the war is over. Google won.*

While I agree with Peter's framing of this upheaval as a culture war, I don't believe the battle lines cleanly divide librarians and computer scientists, and I'm positive it's not over. If we are to know the true nature of this conflict, we must not judge the book by its cover. A recent skirmish serves as case in point. In a *Library Journal* article, Michael Gorman, president-elect of the American Library Association, defined the blog as:

> [An] interactive electronic diary by means of which the unpublishable, untrammeled by editors or the rules of grammar, can communicate their thoughts via the web.

After deriding the "blog people," Gorman then set his sights on "McGoogle":

> Google is, in fact, the device that gives you thousands of "hits" (which may or may not be relevant) in no very useful order....Speed is of the essence to Google boosters...but, as with fast food, rubbish is rubbish, no matter how speedily it is delivered.

After reading this piece, one might write off the entire library profession as a bitter anachronism, but this would be a shame, for the words of Michael Gorman are at odds with the majority of librarians. In fact, many of us were horrified by this high-profile display of ignorance, and some librarian bloggers even called for his resignation.

This unfortunate episode exposed the true fault lines *within* librarianship, and these same divisions exist *within* most other communities and institutions in education, government, health, and business. This is not a contest between librarians and computer scientists, but an ongoing revolution in the definition of authority.

---

* "Search for Tomorrow" by Joel Achenbach. *Washington Post*, February 15, 2004, p. D01. Available at *http://www.washingtonpost.com/ac2/wp-dyn/A42885-2004Feb14?language=printer*.

At one extreme, conservatives cling to traditional views and values, nostalgic for the totalitarian regimes of the Oxford English Dictionary and the Encyclopædia Britannica. In total opposition, liberals embrace the progressive decentralization of the blogosphere, where impious neologisms flourish and the truth is a virus of many colors. And in the middle, the silent majority suffers from information anxiety, trying to allocate trust in a maze of memes where networks supplant hierarchies and fact fades into opinion.

This is a revolution indeed, driven by the design of the Internet, the freedom of speech, and the will of the people. As Lawrence Lessig argues in *The Future of Ideas*, "the defining feature of the Internet is that it leaves resources free."* Its end-to-end architecture locates intelligence at the ends rather than the center, allowing for an innovation commons that's neutral with respect to applications and content.

In the 1990s, this level playing field served as catalyst for the most brilliant period of knowledge creation since the cultural and scientific revolutions of the Renaissance. And in this network culture that sports more web pages than people, we enjoy incredible access to free information. But with freedom comes responsibility, and with free information, finding is not only a right but a duty. In short, access changes the game.

The Body Politic

Findability is at the center of a fundamental shift in the way we define authority, allocate trust, make decisions, and learn independently. There are some visible signs in the rise and fall of bloggers and journalists, search engines and portals, Wikipedia and Britannica, but most of the change comes slow and subtle like poetry, fine wine, and old age.

Consider in this vein, the cards I'm about to show about an episode of back pain I experienced not long ago. While working on this book, and managing a heavy consulting workload, my lower back began to hurt. A lot. I'd had a mild episode the previous year, precipitated by mowing the lawn, but this time it was back with a vengeance.

Since I was spending a lot of time at my desk writing, I first blamed poor posture, and hastily bought an ergonomic Herman Miller chair from OfficeDesigns.com. It's very nice. I'm sitting in it now. But it didn't help my back. After a few weeks of agony, I visited my doctor. I told her that stress could be a factor. She asked me to bend over, told me I have scoliosis, then prescribed physical therapy and three Advil, three times a day.

* *The Future of Ideas* by Lawrence Lessig. Vintage (2002), p. 14.

So now, I'm spending an hour a day on the floor doing the Cat and Camel.* I'm popping 63 pills a week. And my back pain is worse, not better. I've been doing some online research, but the authorities at nih.gov are in agreement with my doctor's course of treatment. So, in desperation, I go to Google. And I enter: "back pain" stress.

I find an article that leads to a book by Dr. John Sarno called *Healing Back Pain: The Mind-Body Connection*, which I instantly buy from Amazon.† Now, I'm not a touchy-feely kinda guy. I've never been to therapy. I'm not into meditation or yoga or crystals. In fact, I've never even had a massage. But I must confess, this book changed my life.

Dr. Sarno's message resonated profoundly with my experience and intuition. In short, he states that the majority of musculoskeletal pain disorders are rooted in repressed emotion. He explains that, in a bid to distract us from anxiety, our autonomic nervous system reduces blood circulation to specific muscles, tendons, or ligaments, thereby causing oxygen deprivation and severe chronic pain. For treatment, he recommends that patients acknowledge the psychosomatic basis and repudiate any structural diagnosis. This means no pills, no physical therapy, and resumption of all normal activity.

I was skeptical at first. Who is this guy? Why should I trust him? Maybe he's just out to sell books. But his evidence and his explanations eventually won me over, and his book mended my back. Dr. John Sarno is a heretic. His theory flies in the face of western medical orthodoxy. In fact, he blames doctors for perpetuating an epidemic of pain that costs our society over a hundred billion dollars a year. And you know what? I believe him. He healed my body. He changed my mind. And I found him on the Internet.

Believe it or not, this is the new face of healthcare. As access to medical information grows, it's increasingly in our best interests to find our own answers. Doctors have little time and a narrow focus. We must take responsibility for ourselves and our loved ones. This is the era of due diligence, informed consent, self-help, and the third opinion.

As we take responsibility for our own decisions, our relationship with authority changes. Doctors can still help us, but they are no longer in control. We are. This is exhilarating and scary. We begin to think differently about doctors and about ourselves. And this transformation extends beyond healthcare into every aspect of our lives, whether we're buying a car or a

---

* See *http://psychologytoday.webmd.com/content/tools/1/slide_basic_stretch.htm* for details.
† *Healing Back Pain: The Mind-Body Connection* by Dr. John E. Sarno. Warner Books (1991).

house or finding a job or a spouse. To not use the data and expert opinions and collective intelligence at our fingertips reeks of personal malpractice. Of course, access doesn't simply require us to make decisions in more areas of our lives. It also changes the game by inviting us to make informed decisions more often.

Let's say you're on vacation in Newport, Rhode Island, shown in Figure 7-2. You're enjoying a relaxing afternoon on the beach, but it's not perfect. It's a bit cloudy. Maybe you should do something else today and hit the beach tomorrow. You whip out your Treo, check the weather forecast, and start exploring things to do. You could tour one of the Newport mansions, or visit one of many museums, historical sites, or lighthouses. You could go shopping downtown or hike along the Cliff Walk. You could rent a bicycle or a motor scooter or a sea kayak. You come across an article about the Green Animals Topiary Garden. It sounds pretty cool. You check Google Maps for directions and distance—a half hour drive. It's a tough decision. Is it worth the trip? Is this the absolute best option? Now your head hurts, but the real pain is in your palm. Maybe it's time for a swim.

Figure 7-2. Newport, Rhode Island

Information Overload

As Calvin Mooers told us back in 1959, people may not want information, because having it can be painful and troublesome. When it comes to information, sometimes less is more, as we see in Figure 7-3. We know this explicitly from studies that show an inverted-U relationship between the volume of information and decision quality. In fact, a recent study at Kings College in London showed that information overload harms concentration more than marijuana.* We also know this tacitly from experience. We have all felt overwhelmed by details, and we all choose, every day of our lives, to ignore vast quantities of data.

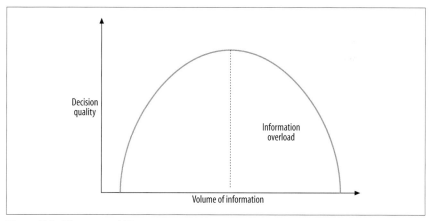

Figure 7-3. The inverted U

We choose not to choose. We rely on habit. We trust familiar brands. We copy our colleagues. But the decisions only multiply faster—education, entertainment, insurance, investment—we are inundated with products, services, plans, and promotions. And it makes us miserable. As Barry Schwartz explains in *The Paradox of Choice*:

> As a culture, we are enamored of freedom, self-determination, and variety.... But clinging tenaciously to all choices available to us contributes to bad decisions, to anxiety, stress, and dissatisfaction—even to clinical depression.†

And the results are not good. Consider the following statistics: according to a National Institutes of Health study, in 1997, the U.S. public spent $36–$47 billion on the complementary and alternative medicines and therapies

---

* "Info-overload harms concentration more than marijuana." *New Scientist*, April 30, 2005, p. 6. Available at *http://www.newscientist.com/channel/being-human/mg18624973.400*.

† *The Paradox of Choice: Why More Is Less* by Barry Schwartz. Ecco (2005), p. 3.

listed in Figure 7-4.* Of this amount, $12–$20 billion was paid out of pocket, including $5 billon on herbal products.

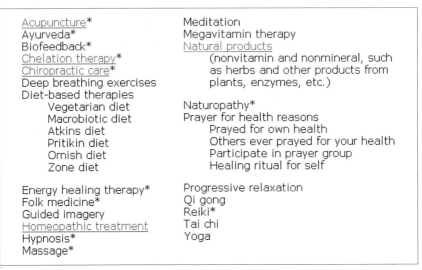

Acupuncture*
Ayurveda*
Biofeedback*
Chelation therapy*
Chiropractic care*
Deep breathing exercises
Diet-based therapies
    Vegetarian diet
    Macrobiotic diet
    Atkins diet
    Pritikin diet
    Ornish diet
    Zone diet

Energy healing therapy*
Folk medicine*
Guided imagery
Homeopathic treatment
Hypnosis*
Massage*

Meditation
Megavitamin therapy
Natural products
    (nonvitamin and nonmineral, such
    as herbs and other products from
    plants, enzymes, etc.)

Naturopathy*
Prayer for health reasons
    Prayed for own health
    Others ever prayed for your health
    Participate in prayer group
    Healing ritual for self

Progressive relaxation
Qi gong
Reiki*
Tai chi
Yoga

Figure 7-4. Complementary and alternative medicines (NCCAM, http://nccam.nih.gov/news/camsurvey_fs1.htm)

That's a lot of money, particularly when it comes on top of the $1.5 trillion we already spend on health insurance, doctor's visits, and prescription medicines. In spite of my recent awakening to the power of mind-body, my guess is that more than half of this money is wasted, though I must admit I'm not certain which half. Or perhaps people are simply paying a high price for the placebo effect. In any event, what we're witnessing is a divergence of beliefs, as information and decision overload induces stress-related problems while simultaneously reducing our ability to identify and manage root causes.

Because our trust in authority has eroded, we must find our own solutions. We select our sources. We choose our news. But since we're swimming in information, our decision quality is poor. So, how do we stop from drowning? We fall back on instinct. We retreat from data. We drop pull and endure push. We pay attention only to messages that find us. And when we do search, we skim. A keyword or two into Google, a few good hits, and we're done. We satisfice with reckless abandon, waffling back and forth between too much information and not enough. And, we make some very bad decisions as individuals, organizations, and societies. But wait. It gets worse. You don't know the half of it.

---

* National Center for Complementary and Alternative Medicines (NCCAM), *http://nccam.nih.gov/news/camsurvey_fs1.htm.*

Graffiti Theory

We're starting to understand the pathology of information consumption and its long-term effects on decisions, thanks to novel insights flowing once again from AI. Our guide to this part of the maze is Jeff Hawkins, founder of Palm Computing and Handspring, architect of the Palm Pilot and Treo, and inventor of an alphabet called Graffiti, shown in Figure 7-5.

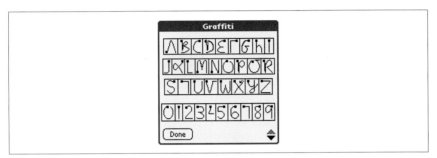

Figure 7-5. Graffiti by Jeff Hawkins

He has made great contributions to mobile computing, yet our interest lies not in Jeff's past but in his passion, which he confesses in his book *On Intelligence*:

> I am crazy about brains. I want to understand how the brain works, not just from a philosophical perspective...but in a detailed nuts and bolts engineering way. My desire is not only to understand what intelligence is and how the brain works, but how to build machines that work the same way. I want to build truly intelligent machines.[*]

Jeff argues that "AI suffers from a fundamental flaw in that it fails to adequately address what intelligence is or what it means to understand something."[†] His quest for understanding has led him, through the fields of computer science, biophysics, linguistics, and neurophysiology, to an intense focus on the neocortex:

> A thin sheet of neural tissue that envelops most of the older parts of the brain...Almost everything we think of as intelligence—perception, language, imagination, mathematics, art, music, and planning—occurs here. Your neocortex is reading this book.[‡]

---

[*] *On Intelligence* by Jeff Hawkins with Sandra Blakeslee. Times Books (2004), p. 1.

[†] Hawkins, p. 13.

[‡] Hawkins, p. 40.

And Jeff's path-breaking work at the Redwood Neuroscience Institute has led to a new model of intelligence, the memory-prediction framework:

> The brain doesn't compute the answers to problems; it retrieves the answers from memory…the entire cortex is a memory system. It isn't a computer at all.[*]

The neocortex stores hierarchical sequences of patterns in invariant form, and recalls those patterns auto-associatively. This lets us recall complete patterns when given only partial or distorted inputs. In the reflection of a flawed ring, we see Plato's perfect circle. In the myriad breeds of canine familiaris, we recognize the category of dog and the tree of Animalia, Chordata, Mammalia. And in three notes, we find the words to a song.

Of course, memory is only half the story. Its conclusion lies in the future:

> Our brains use stored memories to constantly make predictions about everything we see, feel, and hear…what we perceive is a combination of what we sense and of our brains' memory-derived predictions.…Prediction is not just one of the things your brain does. It is the primary function of the neocortex, and the foundation of intelligence.[†]

Jeff argues convincingly that when we take a step, catch a ball, read a poem, or write a book, we draw upon experience to make predictions. We use the past to see the future. Input begets output. Information shapes behavior. Which brings our train of thought back to graffiti, in the form of illegal art on the streets and subways of New York City, shown in Figure 7-6.

Figure 7-6. New York City subway graffiti (The graffiti epidemic in full swing. September 1980. Photo by Steve Zabel, collection of Joe Testagrose. From http://www.nycsubway.org/)

In the *Tipping Point*, Malcolm Gladwell explains the remarkable drop in crime rates in the Big Apple during the 1990s—in five years, total crime fell by 50%, murder by 65%—as evidence that little things can make a big

[*] Hawkins, p. 68.
[†] Hawkins, p. 89.

difference. Specifically, he makes the case for the power of environmental context under the rubric of "broken windows" theory:

> If a window is broken and left unrepaired, people walking by will conclude that no one cares and no one is in charge. Soon, more windows will be broken, and the sense of anarchy will spread....In a city, relatively minor problems like graffiti...are the equivalent of broken windows, invitations to more serious crimes.[*]

In other words, exposure to seemingly insignificant misdemeanors over time can forge a psyche more prone to violent crime. Gladwell uses the 1984 shooting of four unarmed teenagers on the NYC subway by Bernhard Goetz as a case in point. Goetz's split second decision to shoot in "self-defense" resulted from years in an atmosphere of pervasive lawlessness. As his biographer notes, the bullets were "aimed at targets that existed as much in his past as in the present." Input begets output. Information shapes behavior.

Which brings us to graffiti theory, my corollary to both memory-prediction and broken windows, which suggests that all information that flows through our senses continuously and unconsciously shapes our memories, beliefs, predictions, decisions, and behaviors. We are born with instinct, but in matters of intuition, we are lifetime learners. Information is data that makes a difference, literally. It changes our minds, physically.

This is why I feel a twist in my gut when I think about today's standard information fare. At a time when the old-line media of newspapers, radio, and TV broadcast outlets are controlled by a handful of corporations, there's enormous potential for folded feedback, as the predictions of a few become input for the many. We know this from research:

> People mistook the pervasiveness of newspaper stories about homicides, accidents, or fires—vivid, salient, and easily available to memory—as a sign of the frequency of the events these stories profiled. This distortion causes us to miscalculate dramatically the various risks we face in life, and thus contributes to some very bad choices....When you hear the same story everywhere you look and listen, you assume it must be true.[†]

And, we're seeing it already in the growing polarization of beliefs, as we become victims of repetition and rhetoric. Politics shifts gears from differing opinions to different matters of fact. Medicine gets co-opted by drug sellers and spin doctors. Evolution is just a theory, like global warming and weapons of mass destruction. It's hard to find the truth, especially in a *Super Size Me* culture slap happy on soft think and content nuggets.

---

[*] Gladwell, p. 141.
[†] Schwartz, p. 60–61.

But if you look real hard, you can find the truth, or at least that's the theory driving Steven Levitt, one of the world's most brilliant and unusual economists. Levitt's bizarre curiosity, along with a gift for regression analysis, makes him a perfect candidate for exposing the untruths of conventional wisdom. For example, he really turned heads in 2003 by proving that "If you both own a gun and have a swimming pool in the backyard, the swimming pool is about 100 times more likely to kill a child than the gun is."[*]

Levitt's real passion is crime, and his search for answers leads us back to the "broken windows" of New York City. He studied the same crime drop as Malcolm Gladwell, but Levitt's investigation went deeper and wider. Crime rates did indeed fall precipitously in the 1990s, but the trend began *before* the police cleaned up New York City, and similar drops occurred simultaneously in cities throughout the United States. Nationwide, nonviolent crime fell by 40% and the teenage murder rate fell by 50%.

So, it's unlikely that policing strategies in New York City deserve much credit. And, one by one, Levitt proves most of the other popular explanations to be false as well.

Crime-drop explanation	Number of citations in major newspapers[a]
1. Innovative policing strategies	52
2. Increased reliance on prisons	47
3. Changes in crack and other drug markets	33
4. Aging of the population	32
5. Tougher gun control laws	32
6. Strong economy	28
7. Increased number of police	26
8. All other explanations	34

[a] Crime-drop explanations cited in articles published from 1991 to 2001 in the 10 largest-circulation papers in the LexisNexis database. Adapted from *Freakonomics*, p. 120.

So, how does he explain it? In a word, abortion. Levitt argues that the U.S. Supreme Court's 1973 ruling in Roe v. Wade, which legalized abortion, resulted in an immediate decrease in unwanted children, which led to the drop in teenage criminal activity 15 years later. Steven Levitt makes a powerful case. It's certainly hard to dispute his data. And yet, his truth is an uncomfortable one. This is the type of information Calvin Mooers knew people may not want. This is the kind of news that *the many* may choose to ignore.

[*] *Freakonomics* by Steven D. Levitt and Stephen J. Dubner. HarperCollins (2005), p. 146.

The power of our culture and our surrounding information environment to mold us is nothing new. As Herbert Simon noted:

> A man does not live for months or years in a particular position in an organization, exposed to some streams of communication, shielded from others, without the most profound effects upon what he knows, believes, attends to, hopes, wishes, emphasizes, fears, and proposes.[*]

But what is new is the level of control we each have over our sources of input. And the Web, in particular, provides access to myriad sources of news, opinion, and data from all over the world. Google News delivers Aljazeera.net, Blogcritics.org, and CNN.com. A standard keyword search opens the widest of windows on the narrowest of topics. We have the power to inform ourselves like never before. We can manage our information diet, and thus the health and well-being of our rational and intuitive decisions.

So, when it comes to the problem of uninformed decisions, I'd like to say the Web is the solution, but that would be only a half truth, for it can just as easily perpetuate ignorance. In addition to a bias for free and digital, power laws and preferential attachment create dominant hubs and fragmented discussion. A few companies and people capture most of the eyeballs. And in this realm of high precision and low recall, only 15% of web pages include links to opposing viewpoints.[†] Internet topology features countless islands of discourse, isolated by social structure and semantics. For those without a compass, these islands become breeding grounds for misinformation and apophenia.

It's at these degrees of confluence, where information feeds ignorance, that you'll find librarians ranting about literacy. As experts in the critical selection, evaluation, and use of information, we're worried by people's preference for the Web over the library. We're concerned by users who ignore the influence of advertising on source reliability.[‡] Why search the Web when we've got LexisNexis? Why read blogs when we've got books? Why quote Wikipedia when we've got Encyclopædia Britannica? Why choose Google's graffiti ghetto over our scholarly society? Librarians understand what's at stake, and we fear where we're headed. We're canaries in the coal mine, singing a familiar refrain:

> Information literacy is no longer just a library issue.
>
> It is the critical issue for the twenty-first century.[§]

---

[*] Surowiecki, p. 42.

[†] Barabasi, p. 170.

[‡] "Researching and Shaping Information Literacy Initiatives in Relation to the Web" by John Buschman and Dorothy Warner. *The Journal of Academic Librarianship*, vol. 31, no. 1, p. 15.

[§] "Information literacy, a worldwide priority for the twenty-first century" by Ilene Rockman (2003). *Reference Services Review*, vol. 31, no. 3: Research Library, p. 209.

Some heed our warning. For instance, a United Nations declaration puts:

> Information literacy squarely at the center of effective participation in an information society and on equal footing with the educational basics of the 3-Rs.[*]

And, to some extent, information literacy is being incorporated into K–12 education, where it can make the greatest impact. But today, in truth, most people don't listen. Librarians are like doctors, preaching what's good for us, while breaking their own rules. They use Google profusely and rarely speak Boolean. And, in any case, they're not speaking with one voice. In fact, the Internet only makes the fault lines more pronounced.

I, for instance, lean toward the liberal side of librarianship. I see bias in the facts of the *Wall Street Journal* and the Encyclopædia Britannica, and I find real value in the opinion of blogs and the collaboratively authored free content of the Wikipedia. Like relevance, authority is subjective and ascribed by the viewer. Thus, I believe our society needs better information literacy, but I'm not sure we have yet built the understanding or consensus requisite to teach. And, I'm sure that when push comes to shove, access trumps literacy. Information that's hard to find will remain information that's hardly found.

In this sense, it's ironic that in the process of writing this book, my first visit to a physical library was to find the last article, "Rational Choice and the Structure of the Environment" by Herbert Simon. For most of my research, I found what I needed from where I sit, via the free Web, online databases, and my personal bookshelf. But this ancient text wasn't available online, not for free or for fee. So, I was forced to visit the University of Michigan Graduate Library in search of *Psychological Review*, Vol. 63, No. 2, 1956.

This arduous task took a couple of hours, and it wasn't easy, though the thin white line shown in Figure 7-7 was a helpful guide as I negotiated the maze of books to BF1.P7 in the South Stacks on the eighth floor, where I promptly snapped up the article with the camera in my Treo.

And, as I liberated the words of Herbert Simon from their dusty bindings, it occurred to me that the next hands to touch this crumbling text would be working at the behest of Google to digitize all seven million volumes in this canonical library collection.

And, I found myself, once again, inspired by the ambition of Larry Page and Sergey Brin to organize the world's information and make it universally accessible and useful, for these are not just words, but ideas linked to actions with profound social impact.

---

[*] Buschman and Warner, p. 13.

Figure 7-7. The University of Michigan Graduate Library

I can't imagine how anyone who cares about learning and literacy could not be excited by the goals of Google's Library Project, which are summed up as follows:

> This project's aim is simple: help maintain the preeminence of books and libraries in our increasingly Internet-centric culture by making these information resources an integral part of the online experience. We hope to guide more users to their local libraries; to digital archives of some of the world's greatest research institutions; and to out-of-print books they might not be able to find anywhere else—all while carefully respecting authors' and publishers' copyrights.*

The collections of the University of Michigan, Harvard University, Stanford University, the New York Public Library, and Oxford University will be accessible to anyone, any time, anywhere. This is amazing. The world's greatest works of art, history, science, engineering, law, and literature are about to join the conversation we call the Web. Through the lens of graffiti theory, this is a major upgrade to our collective memory, which will ultimately shape our predictions, decisions, and actions. In the end, computers are not about the creation of artificial minds, but the augmentation of real intelligence.

And, our networks are not just about cold hard facts and frictionless data streams, for it's the inspiration in information that separates man from machine. This is why I love the Web. It opens a door to a garden of forking paths, a labyrinth of symbols, wild with ideas and memories and myriad futures present. The Web lets us find our own way. We choose our links and our leaders. We decide where to go, what to believe, and who to follow. Our garden is a maze of heroes and memes, where what we find shapes who we become. Sadly, our story nears its end, but before we part, let's wander through a few more sites and sources that reflect the pregnant promise of ambient findability.

---

* Google Print, Library Project, *http://print.google.com/googleprint/library.html.*

Sources of Inspiration

Given enough eyeballs, all bugs are shallow—this is the conclusion of Eric S. Raymond's anatomy of open source, *The Cathedral and the Bazaar*, which begins with the words:

> Linux is subversive. Who would have thought...that a world-class operating system could coalesce as if by magic out of part-time hacking by several thousand developers scattered all over the planet, connected only by the tenuous strands of the Internet?[*]

Eric explores the evolutionary advantage of self-correcting systems populated by selfish agents over the centralized, top-down approach of traditional software development. At face value, this is a technical essay, but beneath the surface, lies a manifesto.

> Many people (especially those who politically distrust free markets) would expect a culture of self-directed egoists to be fragmented, territorial, wasteful, secretive, and hostile. But this expectation is clearly falsified by (to give just one example) the stunning variety, quality and depth of Linux documentation.[†]

Eric advances open source culture—"release early and often, delegate everything you can, be open to the point of promiscuity"—over the closed models of commerce, positioning Linus Torvald's developing success as evidence that cathedrals must give way to bazaars.

We hear this same rebel yell in the ancient markets of the cluetrain manifesto, the mobile thumb tribes of smart mobs, and the disruptive technologies of peer-to-peer. We embrace the hidden power of social networks and the emergent wisdom of crowds. We are small pieces loosely joined in persistent disequilibrium, gloriously and gladly out of control.

In celebration of the network era, each of these colorful texts makes an impact and then fades into the rich tapestry of our history and culture. With revolutionary fervor, these authors cheer the end of hierarchy, even as their words accrue the ponderous weight of authority, for they forget that today's curators are yesterday's rebels.

The new world of open source and emerging technology has more in common with the old world of libraries and print than we may think. As Lawrence Lessig reminds us, the Oxford English Dictionary was "mankind's first large-scale collaborative open source text project,"[‡] and its

---

[*] "The Cathedral and the Bazaar" by Eric S. Raymond (1998). *First Monday*, vol. 3. no. 3. Available at *http://www.firstmonday.org/issues/issue3_3/index.html*.

[†] Raymond (1998).

[‡] Lessig, p. 19.

---

nascent inclusion of Internet vocabulary, shown in Figure 7-8, suggests it's not dead yet.

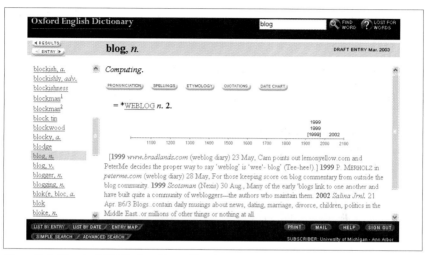

Figure 7-8. Blog in OED Online (Date Chart)

And the free public library was once only a twinkle in the eye of a rebel named Benjamin Franklin. Fifty years before co-authoring and signing the Declaration of Independence, shown in Figure 7-9, young Benjamin created "social libraries" to promote the free sharing of books and the pursuit of knowledge through study and vigorous debate.[*]

Libraries and the Internet have analagous histories, but more important, they represent shared values. Privacy, intellectual freedom, free expression, free and equal access to ideas and information, resistance to censorship— these principles, these unalienable rights and self-evident truths, are held in common by librarians and hackers, from the most revered universities to the most irreverent activists of social software and open source.

This is important, because as Kevin Kelly explains, the people of the book and the people of the screen will soon be on the same page, literally if not figuratively.[†] Not only will we surf the Web on our televisions and watch television on our Treos, but soon digital ink will render it all together on the soft, flexible pages of portable, sharable books.

---

[*] *History of Libraries in the Western World* by Michael H. Harris. Scarecrow Press (1995), p. 183– 184.

[†] "Will We Still Turn Pages?" by Kevin Kelly. *Time Magazine*, June 19, 2000. Available at *http:// www.kk.org/writings/time_turn_pages.php.*

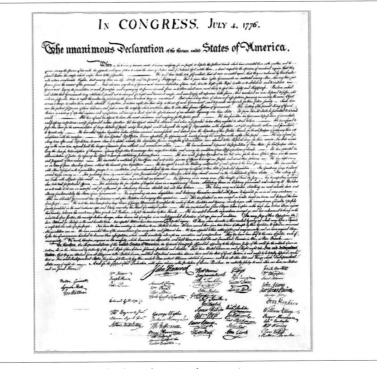

Figure 7-9. The Declaration of Independence (archives.gov)

This is important, because as we shape this bizarre commons of code and content, we can learn much from the cathedrals of knowledge we call libraries. Brewster Kahle, founder of the Internet Archive, understood this earlier than most. In the 1980s, Brewster studied artificial intelligence with Marvin Minsky and helped grow the supercomputer firm, Thinking Machines. Then, in 1992, with the open source releases of WAIS, Brewster included an article on the "Ethics of Digital Librarianship," in which he wrote:

> As digital librarian, you should serve and protect each patron as if she were your only employer. As more of us become involved in serving information electronically...[we] must become conscious of our ethical responsibilities... being a good digital librarian is a concrete way to create a future we all want to live in.[*]

His belief that values must accompany value is evident in the mission of the Internet Archive, to build a digital library that provides universal access to human knowledge:

---

[*] "Ethics of Digital Librarianship" by Brewster Kahle. Available at *http://www.archive.org/about/ethics_BK.php*.

Libraries exist to preserve society's cultural artifacts and to provide access to them...without cultural artifacts, civilization has no memory and no mechanism to learn from its successes and failures...[we are] working to prevent the Internet...and other born-digital materials from disappearing into the past.*

Brewster Kahle's trip began at the center of AI, but his decisions led inevitably to the soft edges of human knowledge. Herbert Simon's search for intelligent machines resulted in the death of decision trees and the birth of bounded rationality. And Jeff Hawkins's quest spawned novel insights into memory, prediction, and the nature of real intelligence. As the footsteps of these wanderers suggest, the journey transforms the destination.

My travels have included many such roundabouts, strange loops, and tangled hierarchies. For example, my fascination with artificial intelligence, back in the summer of 1989, sparked an interest in computers, which led me to computer networks, information science, librarianship, the Internet, and information architecture. My search for AI in the hills of England evolved into a quest for IA among the trees of Ann Arbor, shown in Figure 7-10.†

Figure 7-10. From the hills of England to the trees of Ann Arbor

And my career in information architecture has kindled my passion for findability, which coincidentally led me to write (and you to read) this book. Our paths have crossed at the strange conjunction of ambient findability, and our destinations may never be the same.

---

* "About the Internet Archive" at *http://www4.archive.org/about/about.php*.

† With more than 33,000 trees along its streets, Ann Arbor is known as Tree City, USA.

Ambient Findability

The first person to discover that light contains color was a man named Isaac who grew up on a farm in England roughly 350 years ago. By refracting sunlight with a small triangular prism he bought at Stourbridge Fair, Isaac proved that white light is not homogenous, as natural philosophers since Aristotle had believed, but holds within it the full spectrum of the rainbow. This revolutionary thinker later became Sir Isaac Newton, president of the Royal Society, father of calculus and universal gravitation, and author of *Principia* (Figure 7-11), by common consent the greatest scientific book ever written.

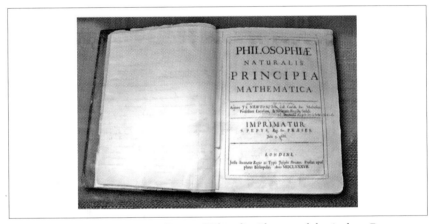

Figure 7-11. Newton's Principia (Source: Wikipedia. Photograph by Andrew Dunn. Creative Commons Attribution ShareAlike 2.0 License)

But it was Newton's early work on colour and the reflecting telescope that enlightens us today, for in his legacy, we learn that now and then we must look away to see. Memory and vision are linked in a dance of senses to an ambient rhythm, and in a very real sense, we all groove to the beat of ambient music, described by the Wikipedia as:

> A loosely defined musical genre that incorporates elements of a number of different styles—including jazz, electronic music, new age, rock and roll, modern classical music, reggae, traditional, world and even noise. It is chiefly identifiable as having an overarching atmospheric context....The term was first coined by Brian Eno...to refer to music that would envelop the listener without drawing attention to itself....Often listeners will forget they are listening to ambient music, which is one of the biggest attractions.[*]

---

[*] "Ambient Music" in the Wikipedia, *http://en.wikipedia.org/wiki/Ambient_music.*

In this text, we've studied the Web through the prism of findability, and gained insight into the future of ubicomp, the evolution of belief, and the enveloping nature of culture. Our amazing journey to ambient findability is well underway. The Web has changed how we live, when we work, where we go, and what we believe. And we ain't seen nothing yet. We can glimpse what lies ahead in the eyes of a child through the lens of a Treo. A brilliant intertwingling of atoms, bits, push, pull, social, semantic, mind, and body, where what we find changes who we become. As Jorges Luis Borges promised us, in the "Garden of Forking Paths," the book and the labyrinth are one and the same. Safe travels.

Index

A

Aboriginal Australians' Songlines, 22
administrative metadata, 126
advertising
    ambient (see ambient advertising)
    SEA (search engine advertising), 112
AI (artificial intelligence)
    decision trees, 155
    introduction, 155
    Simon, Herbert, 156
Alexander, Christopher, 31
Amazon, documents and, 149
ambient advertising, 98
ambient, definition, 6
Ambient Devices, 2, 90
ambiguity of language, 51
American Library Association,
        information literacy and, 8
Anderson, Chris, The Long Tail, 12
ants
    Cataglyphis ants, 18
    geocentric/egocentric navigation, 18
Aristotle, honeybee navigation, 20
Arthur, Paul, 28
as the crow flies, 22
AT&T's Find People Nearby, 84
awards, 10

B

Baldwin, James Mark, 41
    The Baldwin Effect, 41

Barabasi, Albert-Laszlo, 143
Bates, Marcia J., 59–62
battery power, mobile
        communications, 68
bell curves, 52
Berners-Lee, Tim
    Semantic Web and, 121
    W3C, 121
berrypicking techniques, 59
Blair, David C., 50
boundary objects
    Internet as, 119
    Star, Susan Leigh, 119
bounded irrationality, 158
BrailleNote GPS, 76
Brand, Stewart, pace layering, 139
Bray, Tim, 132
bricks, Tangible Media Group, 91
Briet, Suzanne, documents, 148
Brin, David, surveillance and, 95
broken windows theory, 169
browsers
    graphical, 37
    Mosaic, 49
Bush, Vannevar, 34
business value of findability, 8
buying power, marketing and, 103

C

cameras, 86
Card, Stuart, 60
Cataglyphis ants, 18

We'd like to hear your suggestions for improving our indexes. Send email to *index@oreilly.com*.

G

Garrett, Jesse James, folksonomies
    and, 137
genres of communication, 145
    digital genre, 146
    new, 145
geocentric navigation, 18
geocoding, J.C. Spohrer, 75
geofences, 80
Georgia Tech's Smart Floor, 89
Gershon, Nahum, 58
Gibson, William, 3
    cyberspace, 35
GIS (geographic information
    systems), 26
Gladwell, Malcolm
    crime rates study, 168
    irrationality and, 157
glasses, cell phones and, 93
GOMS (Goals, Operators, Methods and
    Selections), 59
Google Maps, 74
Google PageRank, 53
Googlebombing, 152
Gopher, 119
Gorman, Michael, network cultures
    and, 161
gossip, 57
GPS (Global Positioning System), 71
    BrailleNote GPS, 76
    cell phones, law enforcement
        and, 80
    child locator, 78
    chip, 2
    covert tracking, 81
    Digital Angel, 80
    geofences, 80
    Hertz NeverLost, 72
    Networkcar, 80
    OnStar, 80
    personal locator devices, 80
Graffiti, 167–173
graffiti theory, crime and, 169
grapevine, 57
graphical browsers, 37
Greenfield, Adam, 70

H

Habitat, 35
Hawking, Stephen, 95
Hawkins, Jeff, 167
Hayashi, Alden, decision-making
    and, 158
HCI (Human Computer
    Interaction), 59
healthcare
    Digital Angel GPS device, 80
    medical information online, 163
    surveillance, 90
Hendler, James, Semantic Web
    and, 121
Hertz NeverLost navigation system, 72
HII (Human Information
    Interaction), 58
hippocampus, 32
    MRI and, 32
    PET scans and, 32
honeybee navigation, 20
HTML metadata, 132
Huang, Jeffrey, convergent
    architecture, 92
human wayfinding, natural habitats, 20
hypermedia, Ted Nelson and, 64
hypertext, Ted Nelson and, 64

I

information
    communication and, 47
    defining, 45–48
    definition, 46
    marketing and, 103
information foraging, 60
information interaction, 58–63
information literacy, 7–8
information overload, 165–166
information retrieval, 48–51
    users and, 54
informed decisions, 159
Intel, Gordon Moore and, 43
intertwingling
    imports and, 86–90
intertwingularity, 64
    Nelson, Ted and, 64
iProspect, search engines and, 112

irrationality
  bounded irrationality, 158
  decision-making and, 157
  Gladwell, Malcolm, 157
Ishii, Hiroshi, 91

J

Johnson, Steven, 56
Juhnke, Deborah, documents and, 144

K

Kahle, Brewster, digital librarianship
    and, 176
Kelly, Kevin, 175
keyboards, Twiddler, 69
keyword searches, 4
King, Andy, user experience and, 110
knowledge, definition, 46
Kotler, Philip, 113

L

labyrinths, 16
Lakoff, George, 33
  taxonomies and, 129
landmarks
  environmental legibility, 27
  visual, 18
language
  ambiguity, 51
  controlled vocabularies, 53
  representation and, 51
  words, 51
Lassila, Ora, Semantic Web and, 121
Laws, Kevin, 13
laws of Moore and Mooers, 43
Lessig, Lawrence, network cultures
    and, 162
Levitt, Steven, broken window theory
    and, 170
lighthouses, 22
Linnaean taxonomy of living
    things, 127
location
  Google Maps, 74
  MapQuest, 74
location-sensing devices
  BrailleNote GPS, 76
  covert tracking devices, 81

Degree Confluence Project and, 76
Digital Angel, 80
geofences, 80
Mappr, 76
OnStar, 80
personal locator, 80
social software services, 84
Wherify Wireless GPS Personal
    Locator, 78
location-sensing techniques, 73
Loran, 26
Lost and Found, 13
lumitouch, Tangible Media Group, 91
Lyman, Peter, network cultures
    and, 161
Lynch, Kevin, 17, 26

M

magnetic map, sea turtles, 20
Mann, Steve, convergence, 93
Mappr, photography and, 76
MapQuest, 74
maps, 24–26
  Gerardus Mercator, 26
  Google Maps, 74
  Mapquest, 74
marketing, 101
  buying power and, 103
  definition, 102
  information and, 103
  variety and, 103
Maron, M.E., 50
mazes, 16
McCullough, Malcolm, physical and
    digital architecture, 92
medical information online, 163
Mercator, Gerardus, Mercator
    Projection, 26
Merholz, Peter, genres of
    communication, 147
metadata
  administrative, 126
  Amazon and, 149
  descriptive, 126
  Google and, 53
  HTML and, 132
  RDF and, 131, 132
  structural, 126
  tags, 53

About the Author

Peter Morville is widely recognized as a founding father of the emerging field of information architecture, and he serves as a passionate advocate for the critical role that findability plays in defining the user experience. Peter is coauthor (with Louis Rosenfeld) of the best-selling book on the subject, *Information Architecture for the World Wide Web*, named "Best Internet Book of 1998" by Amazon and "The Most Useful Book on Web Design on the Market" by usability guru Jakob Nielsen. Peter's work and ideas have been featured in numerous publications, including *Business Week*, the *Economist*, the *Wall Street Journal*, MSNBC, and *Fortune*.

Colophon

Our look is the result of reader comments, our own experimentation, and feedback from distribution channels. Distinctive covers complement our distinctive approach to technical topics, breathing personality and life into potentially dry subjects.

The animal on the cover of *Ambient Findability* is a Verreaux's sifaka (*Propithecus verreauxi*). A rare lemur found only in Madagascar, the sifaka spends most of its time in trees, feeding on fruit, flowers, wood, bark, and leaves.

Two unusual traits distinguish sifakas from other lemurs. First, when threatened, a sifaka lets out a loud alarm call that sounds like *shi-fak*—this odd barking sound is where the animal gets its name. Second, the sifaka is known for its famous dance. Because the trees in the sifaka's habitat are spread out, it is sometimes forced to move across the ground from tree to tree. During these brief earthbound trips, the sifaka bipedally hops sideways and wildly waves its arms in the air. Extremely vulnerable on the ground, sifakas use this "dancing" to ward off predators.

Adam Witwer was the production editor and Linley Dolby was the copyeditor for *Ambient Findability*. Ann Atalla proofread the text. Colleen Gorman and Claire Cloutier provided quality control. Johnna VanHoose Dinse wrote the index.

Karen Montgomery designed the cover of this book, based on a series design by Edie Freedman, and produced the cover layout with Adobe InDesign CS using Adobe's ITC Garamond font. The cover image is from *Cassell's Natural History*.

David Futato designed the interior layout. This book was converted by Keith Fahlgren to FrameMaker 5.5.6 with a format conversion tool created by Erik Ray, Jason McIntosh, Neil Walls, and Mike Sierra that uses Perl and XML technologies. The text font is Linotype Birka; the heading font is Adobe Myriad Condensed; and the code font is LucasFont's TheSans Mono Condensed. The illustrations that appear in the book were produced by Robert Romano, Jessamyn Read, and Lesley Borash using Macromedia Free-Hand MX and Adobe Photoshop CS. The tip and warning icons were drawn by Christopher Bing. This colophon was written by Adam Witwer.

Better than e-books

Try it Free! Sign up today
and get your first 14 days free.
Go to *safari.oreilly.com*

Search
thousands of
top tech books

Download
whole chapters

Cut and Paste
code examples

Find
answers fast

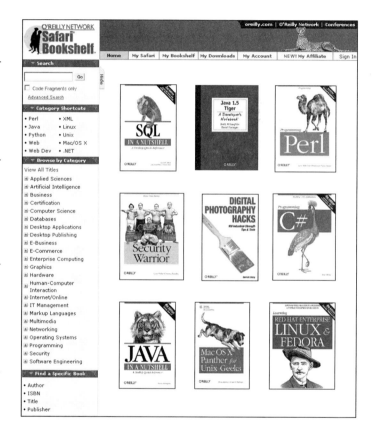

Search Safari! The premier electronic reference
library for programmers and IT professionals.

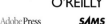

Related Titles from O'Reilly

Web Programming

ActionScript Cookbook

ActionScript for Flash MX: The Definitive Guide, *2nd Edition*

Dynamic HTML: The Definitive Reference, *2nd Edition*

Flash Hacks

Essential PHP Security

Google Hacks, *2nd Edition*

Google Pocket Guide

HTTP: The Definitive Guide

JavaScript & DHTML Cookbook

JavaScript Pocket Reference, *2nd Edition*

JavaScript: The Definitive Guide, *4th Edition*

Learning PHP 5

PayPal Hacks

PHP Cookbook

PHP in a Nutshell

PHP Pocket Reference, *2nd Edition*

PHPUnit Pocket Guide

Programming ColdFusion MX, *2nd Edition*

Programming PHP

Upgrading to PHP 5

Web Database Applications with PHP and MySQL, *2nd Edition*

Webmaster in a Nutshell, *3rd Edition*

Web Authoring and Design

Cascading Style Sheets: The Definitive Guide, *2nd Edition*

CSS Cookbook

CSS Pocket Reference, *2nd Edition*

Dreamweaver MX 2004: The Missing Manual, *2nd Edition*

Essential ActionScript 2.0

Flash Out of the Box

Head First HTML & CSS

HTML & XHTML: The Definitive Guide, *5th Edition*

HTML Pocket Reference, *2nd Edition*

Information Architecture for the World Wide Web, *2nd Edition*

Learning Web Design, *2nd Edition*

Programming Flash Communication Server

Web Design in a Nutshell, *3rd Edition*

Web Site Measurement Hacks

Web Administration

Apache Cookbook

Apache Pocket Reference

Apache: The Definitive Guide, *3rd Edition*

Perl for Web Site Management

Squid: The Definitive Guide

Web Performance Tuning, *2nd Edition*

Our books are available at most retail and online bookstores.

To order direct: 1-800-998-9938 • *order@oreilly.com* • *www.oreilly.com*

Online editions of most O'Reilly titles are available by subscription at *safari.oreilly.com*

Keep in touch with O'Reilly

Download examples from our books

To find example files from a book, go to: *www.oreilly.com/catalog* select the book, and follow the "Examples" link.

Register your O'Reilly books

Register your book at *register.oreilly.com* Why register your books? Once you've registered your O'Reilly books you can:

- Win O'Reilly books, T-shirts or discount coupons in our monthly drawing.
- Get special offers available only to registered O'Reilly customers.
- Get catalogs announcing new books (US and UK only).
- Get email notification of new editions of the O'Reilly books you own.

Join our email lists

Sign up to get topic-specific email announcements of new books and conferences, special offers, and O'Reilly Network technology newsletters at:

elists.oreilly.com

It's easy to customize your free elists subscription so you'll get exactly the O'Reilly news you want.

Get the latest news, tips, and tools

www.oreilly.com

- "Top 100 Sites on the Web"—PC Magazine
- CIO Magazine's Web Business 50 Awards

Our web site contains a library of comprehensive product information (including book excerpts and tables of contents), downloadable software, background articles, interviews with technology leaders, links to relevant sites, book cover art, and more.

Work for O'Reilly

Check out our web site for current employment opportunities:

jobs.oreilly.com

Contact us

O'Reilly Media, Inc.
1005 Gravenstein Hwy North
Sebastopol, CA 95472 USA
Tel: 707-827-7000 or 800-998-9938
    (6am to 5pm PST)
Fax: 707-829-0104

Contact us by email

For answers to problems regarding your order or our products:
order@oreilly.com

To request a copy of our latest catalog:
catalog@oreilly.com

For book content technical questions or corrections: **booktech@oreilly.com**

For educational, library, government, and corporate sales: **corporate@oreilly.com**

To submit new book proposals to our editors and product managers:
proposals@oreilly.com

For information about our international distributors or translation queries:
international@oreilly.com

For information about academic use of O'Reilly books:
adoption@oreilly.com
or visit:
academic.oreilly.com

For a list of our distributors outside of North America check out:
international.oreilly.com/distributors.html

Order a book online

www.oreilly.com/order_new

 ®

Our books are available at most retail and online bookstores.
To order direct: 1-800-998-9938 • *order@oreilly.com* • *www.oreilly.com*
Online editions of most O'Reilly titles are available by subscription at *safari.oreilly.com*